Hang Gliding Handbook–
Fly Like A Bird

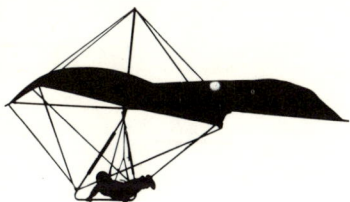

Hang Gliding Handbook–
Fly Like A Bird

By George Siposs

TAB BOOKS
Blue Ridge Summit, Pa. 17214

FIRST EDITION

FIRST PRINTING— JUNE 1975

Copyright ◉ 1975 by TAB BOOKS

Printed in the United States
of America

Hardbound Edition: International Standard Book No. 0-8306-5776-2

Paperbound Edition: International Standard Book No. 0-8306-4776-7

Library of Congress Card Number: 75-1699

About the Author

Sports- and hobby-minded TAB readers are well acquainted with the books written by George Siposs: *Model Car Racing Control; Land Sailing...from RC Models to the Big Ones;* and *Model Sail & Power Boating by Remote Control.*

Mr. Siposs is a professional mechanical engineer with eight patents and hundreds of magazine articles to his credit. He is an ardent hobbyist and winner of numerous awards and trophies. In addition to writing nonfiction books, he is working on a full length novel and teaches professional writing and photograph/ at Golden West College in Southern California.

Contents

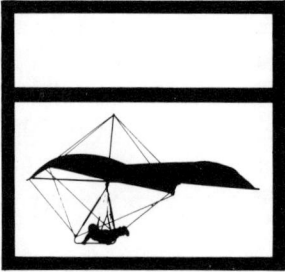

Introduction

It was a pleasant Saturday afternoon in 1973; a balmy breeze was blowing in from the Pacific. As my wife and I walked slowly on the sand at Torrance beach, near Los Angeles, a giant kite-like device left the top of the bluffs above us and floated gently towards the beach. A man was suspended under the contraption! He made a couple of majestic turns and landed almost directly in front of us, a contented smile on his face.

My heart beat a wild rhythm. Could it be? Did I really see a man fly a homemade airplane? Did my childhood dreams suddenly become real? I ran to the man and showered him with questions: "Did you build it? How much did it cost? How many times have you flown it?" The man calmly reached into his back pocket and pulled out a business card. It read: DAVID MUEHL—KITE FLYER.

It *was* true. A manmade, ultralight kite had indeed been flying in front of my eyes. David told me all about this fabulous sport, the people who fly their own kites, and the materials they use.

A few weeks later my son burst into the room when he came home from school; "Dad, you should see my friends fly their homemade airplane in the park." I jumped into my car and rushed out to the nearby park; it had a fair-sized hill used by kids for fast bicycle runs and model airplane flights. As I parked, I saw a huge, black form on top of the hill, silhouetted against the setting sun. It was a dart-shaped, bamboo contraption covered with black plastic. Five young men were holding the wings; another struggled with the middle.

Obviously, he was the pilot-to-be. The boys held the kite against the wind and, as the plastic billowed up, they began to run down the hill. The boy in the middle who hung onto the bamboo frame suddenly lifted his feet. He skimmed over the bushes and dragged along the grass before he landed only a few yards from me. The boy, Ernest Feher, told me that he had been building and flying homemade airplanes for a few months, often quite successfully. His dream was to have a sustained flight, like a bird.

Who hasn't dreamt of flying like a bird? Of being free from the bondage of gravity? *I* sure have. In my childhood I built many model airplanes. The larger ones tugged at my hands when the wind blew directly in my face and I held them on the starting line. I even dreamed about building a plane large enough to lift me up. But, lacking the funds and know-how, I never realized my dream—until last year. The hang gliding movement is going strong in Southern California and is sweeping the nation. There are now well over 10,000 registered hang glider pilots in this country alone. I, too, became caught up in its whirlwind. I visited a flying site and found that some manufacturers of ultralight airplanes actually gave flying lessons to anybody willing to plunk down $25—and who had courage enough to undergo a one-day course of instruction; simple as that.

So I worked up some courage and went out to Escape Country, a park south of Los Angeles where several gentle hills afforded me some enjoyable flights during the months past (some not more than extended hops). I never will be a great exhibition flyer, but I share the exhilaration my companions on the hill experience. Most of them are convinced that hang gliding is the highest high, the ultimate experience, and the last frontier for man.—and the only place one can really feel part of the elements is beneath a free-flying hang glider. Jack Schroeder, one of the experienced fliers, said that some flights actually bring him close to tears.

Hang gliding, now a worldwide sport, is relaxing and healthy. It is ecology-oriented; quiet and clean. It need not involve competition; yet, if you feel the urge to pit yourself against others you can find plenty of opportunities to compete.

My feeling for this sport compelled me to write about it. You may never actually fly a hang glider, or even see one, but I hope that reading about them will almost make you feel the wind in your face, the pull of the control bar, and the satisfaction of a good landing.

As with any new sport, the hang gliding picture is changing constantly. New equipment is being developed, new rules made, new sites opening up, and new faces and names keep appearing. If some of the items presented in this book become outdated too quickly, it will be because the sport is just too dynamic to keep up with. The information presented was, at least, up-to-date as of the end of 1974.

I did not intend this to be a book which can teach hang gliding without an instructor. With this warning, I disclaim any liability for accidents, should the reader have any. My intent here is to present a picture complete enough so that the novice can bring himself up to date in an evening or two. In this manner fewer questions will have to be asked of dealers and instructors. The reader will be able to analyze the flights of others (or his own) in a logical and scientific light. It has been my aim to produce a book that will shorten the learning period and aid in the sane, safe, and controlled growth of hang gliding—with emphasis on a basic human dream: to fly like a bird and experience the joy of freedom.

And, although this book is not a know-it-all, I hope experienced fliers also find it enjoyable.

I wish to thank my friends and those companies who have helped supply material for this book and who gave permission to reprint the illustrations. I am indebted to: Flight Realities, Inc.; Sunbird Gliders; Sport Kites; Chandelle Skysails; Whitney Enterprises; Aerodyne Co.; Manta Wings; Volmer Aircraft; S&F Tool Co.; International Aerospace Hall of Fame; Ultralight Flying Machines; Quest; Solo Flight; Concepts Inc.; Hang Glider Shoppe; Delta Wing Kites; Dwyer Gages; Skycraft, Inc.; Mountain Green Sailwing; Mehil Enterprises; Colver Instruments; Harlan Aircraft; Free Flight Systems; Sun Sail Corp.; WB Products; Conquest; Velderrain Kite Co.; Ultralight Products; Eipper-Formance; as well as Scotty Thom, Ernest Feher, John Worth, Gerald

Albiston, Bob Harlan, Frank Shaffer, Crawford Meeks, Bill Bennett, James Spurgeon, Volmer Jensen, Rob Robinson, Walter Hesse, Frank Zaic, Robbie Skinner, Richard Miller, Eddie Paul, Bob Wills, Jim Foreman, Will Battles, Larry Mauro, Willis Allen, Jack Lambie, Don K. Trimble, Jack Hall, Mike Flannigan, Klaus Hill, Larry Hall, Shannon Adams, Peter Brock, Steve Murray, David Muehl, Jim Roberts, and Earl Manning.

—George G. Siposs

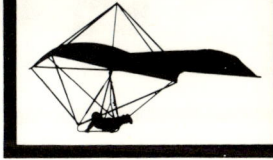

Chapter 1

The History of Hang Gliding

Man has always wanted to be free; free from slavery, free to express himself—free from the bondage of gravity.

Perhaps the earliest recorded attempt to fly can be found in ancient Greek mythology where, it is told, Daedalus and his son Icarus were stranded on the Isle of Crete. Some versions of the myth say that they were imprisoned there and, in a desperate attempt to take flight from his predicament, Daedalus collected large feathers from hawks and attached them to his arms with beeswax. Flapping them up and down, he found that he could actually fly—or so the tale goes (Fig. 1-1). He fashioned similar wings for his son and taught him to fly, warning never to fly too high because the sun will melt the wax. Well, one day they decided to escape and with a mighty leap, they took off. Icarus was absolutely intoxicated with his new ability and kept going higher and higher. Daedalus shouted at him to take heed; but it was too late. The wax melted, the feathers floated to earth, and Icarus plummeted to his death. Once safe in Italy, Daedalus warned all who inquired about his flight to never try flying.

Several hundreds of years later, an inventive Chinese experimenter attached kites to his body and had himself towed aloft. Some say he attached rockets to his body. Whatever the truth may be, he took off; and crash-landed—earning the scorn of those wise enough to remain earthbound.

Around the turn of the fifteenth century Leonardo da Vinci, the famous Italian painter, sculptor, and engineer, made several sketches for a manned flying machine. He patterned his design after bats; he taught his disciples that

Fig. 1-1. Icarus. (Courtesy Free Flight Systems)

this was the best natural model to use. Pictures of the bat-inspired device show it to be made from cane and silk. The pilot was to be strapped to the machine in such a way that flapping the wings and kicking his feet to move the tail would make him fly. We know now that muscle power is scarcely enough to sustain flight, let alone allowing a takeoff by flapping.

During the 19th century there were many attempts at flying, but they all emphasized big, heavy machines driven by engines or lifted aloft by balloons; interesting devices, but not pertinent to the development of hang gliders.

Otto Lilienthal, a German inventor born in 1848, felt the need to fly like a bird—or else he must have been convinced that the future of aviation lay in ultralight flying machines. Before his time there was no reliable knowledge available on the physics of flight, airfoils, aircraft construction, or flying techniques. He had to devise all the basics himself. He used willow wands covered with waxed cloth for wings. He reasoned correctly that air must slide past the cloth instead of penetrating it. He discovered the importance of the airfoil and center of gravity. Writing his findings in dissertations, log books, and patents, he pursued his experiments with traditional German thoroughness and great determination; he even had a huge hill constructed for his experiments. His friends built a shed at the base of the hill where he could store his gliders and tools.

Lilienthal made more than 2000 flights from his hill, covering distances up to a quarter of a mile. He discovered that by shifting his weight he could control his glider's flight

16

path. His first monoplane (Fig. 1-2), built in 1891, had a wing span of 23 feet and weighed just under 50 pounds—comparable to today's hang gliders. A tail was attached to the wing for stability. Later, he found that two wings would give him even greater stability, and more lift. To obtain more precise control, he connected an elevator control to his head. One of his gliders was made collapsible so that it would be easily portable.

Although most of his designs were first tested on the ground, he encountered a gust of wind during a practice session and fell to the ground from a height of 50 feet on August 9, 1896. A day later he died; he had broken his spine during the fall. This great pioneer, who invented all the basic elements of hang gliding, said at the last, "Sacrifices must be made."

Percy Pilcher was one of England's hang glider pioneers. His craft was somewhat similar to Lilienthal's, but the Pilcher machine had more guy (bracing) wires. One of his first designs had a wing loading (Chapter 2) of about 0.7 lb/sq ft of wing area. His later gliders were capable of nearly twice this loading. On a particularly successful day near Eynsford, he rose from a hilltop and flew nearly 300 yards into the valley below. He was hoping to add an engine to his plane, but before this could be realized he suffered a fatal accident caused by one of the wires snapping. He died at Stamford Hill in September of 1899.

Fig. 1-2. The Lilienthal hang glider. (Spurgeon collection)

Fig. 1-3. The Chanute glider—1896. (Spurgeon collection)

On the North American continent, Octave Chanute, distinguished president of the Society of Civil Engineers, had been experimenting with manned flying machines for a number of years. He tried modifications of the original Lilenthal design with minor improvements. Later, he perfected his own designs; some were monoplanes; others, biplanes (Fig. 1-3). Most of his designs incorporated two parallel bars in the center of the wing, which were under his armpits as he flew. Control was by means of shifting his weight. A newspaper account in 1896 states that: "...he has made journeys of 300 feet, reaching at times height of more than 30 feet, and has alighted as easily and gracefully as a bird. When starting from the top of a hill the operator runs a few steps, then the machine rises and proceeds through the air in an almost horizontal position. When he wishes to stop, he tilts his body so that the wings are inclined upward. This checks the speed and the airplane coasts slowly to the ground. The flights are made in the direction from which the wind is blowing..."—and you probably thought hang gliding was a new invention.

The Wright brothers tried to develop an airplane which would carry a pilot in complete safety and comfort. Their gliders had provisions for seating, or for a prone flying position; thus, they are not considered hang gliders in the strictest sense. Their contributions to aeronautical science have, nevertheless, been invaluable.

Now let us backtrack a few years and move to the West Coast of the United States, a nearly deserted land just before the turn of the 20th century. This is what James R. Spurgeon, aviation historian, has to say about one of the pioneers of hang gliding:

> "The world owes the mastery of the air to a man of Catholic faith who firmly believed that he was endowed by God to be the first man to fly. He designed, built, and flew his first glider near San Diego, California on August 28, 1883. This tends to upset the history books a little bit but, nevertheless, John J. Montgomery made man's first successful controlled flight in a machine weighing only 40 pounds and fashioned after the birds he had studied, following Nature's great teachings."

Montgomery was born of pioneer parents at Yuba City, California on February 15, 1858. Since his childhood he was interested in flying; intrigued by Nature's great genius evident in the shape and action of wings, he studied birds.

John attended St. Joseph's grade school in Oakland and went on to St. Mary's High School. During his freshman year at Santa Clara College (1874—75), he took great interest in the science classes taught by Rev. Aloysius Brunengo. He earned his B.S. and M.S. degrees in physics at St. Ignatius College, San Francisco, after studying under the brilliant Rev. Joseph Neri who introduced electric lighting to the city for the centennial celebration of 1876.

John's family moved to a new ranch near Otay (south San Diego) in December 1881; he joined them in the spring of 1882. He set up his workshop and was allowed to use the barn loft for the construction of a flying machine. With the help of his sister Jane, pumping the bellows to fire the steam boiler for fashioning ashwood strips into parabolic, cambered wing-ribs, his dream slowly took the shape of a huge bird.

John's friends and neighbors joshed him about his ambition to fly, but this did not discourage the genius, who knew he would succeed. In the early morning of August 28, 1883, John and his brother James loaded the precious flying craft (Fig. 1-4) onto a frame haywagon and covered it with straw to hide it from the eyes of folk who thought him "tetched." The boys drove off holding rifles as if to suggest they were going rabbit hunting. John had previously selected the site, a gentle hill facing the ocean. After assembling the craft, John stood holding the glider over his head while straddling the bottom center bar of the light fuselage. James tied a rope to the nose of the lower bar and stood ready for John's signal. The breeze picked up and John yelled, "Run!" Taking a few steps, he jumped into the air. "I found myself launched into the air," he wrote; "I proceeded against the wind, gliding downhill for a distance of about 600 feet. In this experience, I was able to direct my course at will. A peculiar sensation came over me, the fact that I was placing myself at the mercy of the wind and, immediately after, came a feeling of security when I realized the solid support given by the wing surfaces. This support was of a very peculiar nature because there was a cushiony softness about it, yet it was firm. When I

Fig. 1-4. Montgonery's 1883 monoplane glider. (Spurgeon collection)

found that the machine would follow my movements in the seat for balancing. I felt I was self-buoyant."

Between 1883 and 1889, John improved his designs and built models to test his theory. Later, he taught physics at Santa Barbara College where he enjoyed the understanding of his associates and their help in his continuing experiments in flight. In October 1901, he took his new monoplane, the *Evergreen*, out in the country southeast of San Jose; after making 55 flights, he made an adjustment on the stabilizer and, upon takeoff, side-slipped to the ground. A stovebolt in the fuselage penetrated his brain—death came an hour later on October 31, 1901.

In May 1909, the Austrian Flying Technical Society, after several years of investigation, named John J. Montgomery the First Man To Fly.

Aviation had its golden days from the 1920s to the 1930s. With the advent of powerful engines, speed and distance records were set. The world wars contributed greatly to the development of fast, reliable planes; it's no wonder that unpowered planes did not receive much publicity. However, at the end of World War I, Germany was prohibited from building powered planes and German aviation enthusiasts turned their attention to gliders. They perfected their planes to a high degree of sophistication. Streamlining became very important, and long, soaring flights took the spotlight. But hang gliders hadn't been completely forgotten.

Francis M. Rogallo, a mechanical engineer, went to work for the Langley Center in 1936. During his years there, he experimented with a variety of aircraft. Going back to basics, he did considerable work on kites as well. Because kites were not considered serious projects at Langley, Rogallo and his wife experimented on their own time. In 1948, they took out a patent (No. 2,546,078) which describes a simple kite with cylindrical wings. The wings kept their curved shape by the movement of air alone. Hence, they were called *limp-wing* kites. After more experimentation, the Rogallos developed a dartlike version of a kite intended for free flight. The National Aeronautics and Space Administration spent millions of dollars developing this shape for a variety of purposes. One was to be used as a parachute with a predictable forward velocity, in addition to a controlled sink speed. It was to be used to allow downed pilots to glide back towards their own troops. Another delta-wing version had inflatable air tubes at the leading edges and keel for additional support. The payload was fastened to the bottom of the kite with a multiplicity of shrouds. The intent for this device was to provide a safe, controlled landing for returning spacecraft. Radio-controlled models were built with rigid leading edges and keel to develop flight characteristics for the Rogallo wing. Again, the intent was to have a vehicle which could be stored, folded in a tube, and erected in midair to provide a safe descent for the payload. But during those years Rogallo wings received little publicity; no one imagined they would form the basis of a popular sport in just a few years.

During the war years, powered planes were prohibited from being built or flown within 150 miles of the California coast. Undaunted, Vollmer Jensen, a California aviation enthusiast, built and flew several ultralight gliders of his own design. He provided the primary flight controls (rudder, elevator, and ailerons), but he still retained the basic hanging position for his planes. During the next 30 years, he and his aerodynamicist friends developed special airfoils and built hang gliders which are still considered "advanced" designs. The Vollmer planes are not only professionally produced, they outfly all other hang gliders in existence today.

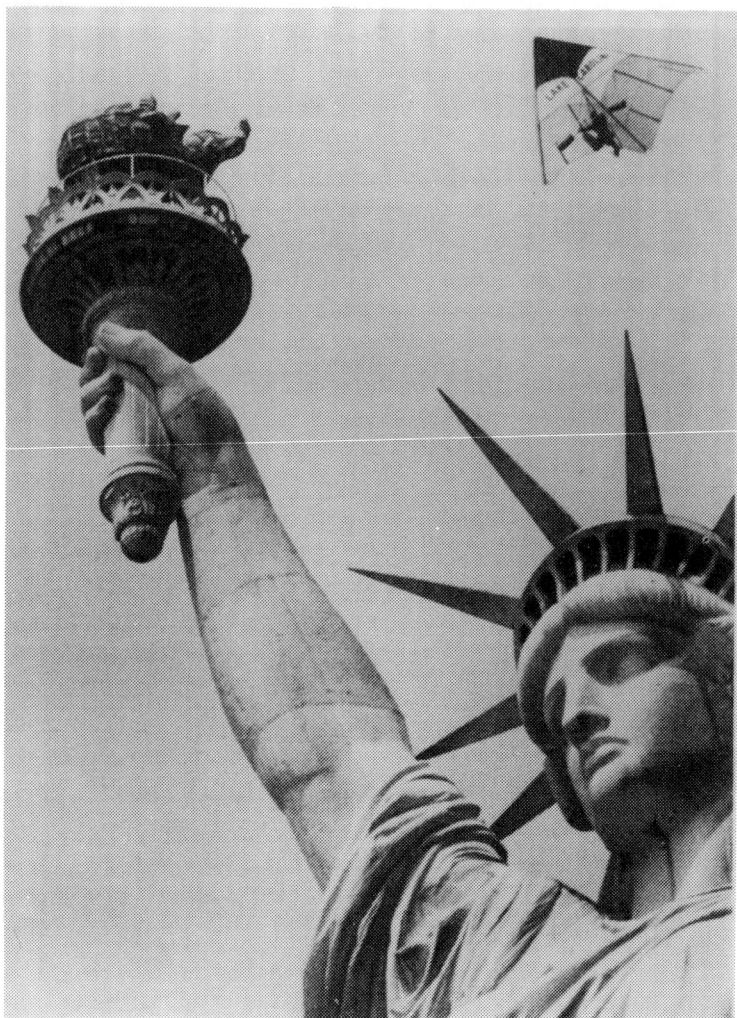

Fig. 1-5. Bill Bennett, Australian birdman, flying above the Statue of Liberty. (Courtesy Delta Wing Kites and Gliders, Inc.)

In 1964, Richard Miller proved that a Rogallo wing could be built inexpensively by fabricating one from bamboo and polyethylene for less than $10. The *Bamboo Butterfly*, as he called it, raised many an eyebrow with its hops and jumps. Nevertheless, it was a true forerunner of the hang gliding sport.

A California school teacher, Jack Lambie has been a glider enthusiast for many years and owns several high-performance gliders. In 1970 he and his students built a bamboo and plastic biplane hang glider. Another major milestone in the development of the sport, the *Hang Loose*, proved that homemade machines can indeed fly and provide fun. Jack Lambie sponsored a hang glider meet in San Diego in 1971—on Lilienthal's birthday—providing the movement with further momentum.

During the early 1960s an intrepid Australian, Bill Bennett, experimented with Rogallo wings. He came to the United States in 1969 and gave several kite-flying demonstrations, making most of his takeoffs from the water after being towed by a boat. After he reached the proper height, he would be cut loose, astounding the spectators with his skill and daring. He flew around the Statue of Liberty (Fig. 1-5) and the Golden Gate bridge (Fig. 1-6). He was either towed behind boats, cars, snowmobiles, and balloons, or he simply took off from hills. For one of his demonstrations, he took off from Dante's View in Death Valley, California (Fig. 1-7). His flight, lasting more than 11 minutes, covered 6.2 miles with a drop in altitude of more than a mile. One of his more noteworthy roles was that of kite-flying instructor to Roger Moore for his part in the James Bond film *Live and Let Die* (Fig. 1-9). (Bennett did the actual stunt flying.)

During earlier days, kite flying was considered a stunt. Bill Bennett was billed as the "Australian Birdman" when he flew into crowded baseball parks, the Ontario Motor Raceway, and other public places. Today Bennett is the president of *Delta Wing Kites and Gliders* in Van Nuys, California. Recently, in honor of his pioneering efforts, he was elected to the National Soaring Hall of Fame.

Hang gliding in the early 1970s was, in the main, considered to be for people with "no respect for safety and a suicide-wish." The public knew little of the tremendous amount of effort and the thousands of flights that went into developing hang gliding as a safe sport. To insure the publicity the sport needed, manufacturers and private individuals set

Fig. 1-6. Bill Bennett soars above the Golden Gate bridge. (Courtesy Delta Wing Kites and Gliders, Inc.)

out to establish world records and demonstrate the reliability of hang gliders. One challenger, Rudi Kishazy, flew from Mont Blanc—at 15,766 ft, one of the tallest peaks in Europe (Fig. 1-9). He went on to make other incredible flights from equally dangerous sites.

As it has been with so many other sports and outdoor activities, Californians led the way in hang gliding. An expert

Fig. 1-7. Bill Bennett takes off from Dante's View in Death Valley. (Courtesy Delta Wing Kites and Gliders, Inc.)

water skier, Dave Kilbourne was one of the early fliers of delta-wing kites (as the Rogallo wing was being called) who was towed aloft behind motor boats. They used small kites; most were around 13 feet in wingspan. Dave tried foot-launching his kite, and was successful. In fact, he is credited with having foot-launched the first swing-seat kite. Early fliers, feeling that their kites were capable of staying aloft for more than just a few minutes, developed simple seats (taken from backyard swings) to save their arms during long flights. Dave launched his 16-foot kite from the top of Mission Ridge on September 6, 1971 for a flight lasting 1 hour 4 minutes.

Taras Kiceniuk, Jr., a 19-year-old Cal Tech student, built a tailless glider he foot-launched from the Torrey Pines cliffs in San Diego, California; he surpassed Kilbourne's duration with a flight of 1 hour 11 minutes.

Fig. 1-8. Roger Moore as James Bond in "Live and Let Die." (Courtesy Delta Wing Kites and Gliders, Inc.)

Bob Wills, a student and part-time salesman for Bill Bennett, had a 19-foot kite built which he flew at Palmdale, California for a duration of 2 hours 16 minutes. Six weeks later, Taras Kiceniuk, Jr. replied with a flight of 2 hours 26 minutes. The race was on.

Bob Wills felt that conditions at Torrey Pines, where regular gliders are provided lift by balmy Pacific breezes hitting the sheer bluffs, were ideal for setting yet another record. He tried his luck and on December 7, 1972 flew his delta-wing kite for 3 hours 3 minutes. Then, on April 13, 1973 Tony Kolerich, a 19-year-old student, beat the record. Tony had heard about hang gliding during his high-school days. He and his friends built a bamboo-and-plastic contraption, and later he graduated to more advanced models, flying one for 3 hours 9 minutes. He had just gotten up in the air, and was having great fun, when one by one the other fliers landed—but he stayed up there! Darkness fell, but the lift seemed everlasting. Tony flew back and forth over the beach homes, waving and talking to people having candlelit backyard dinners near the site. His sail, black plastic, was nearly invisible. Tony was exhausted and cold, and the seat ropes cut into his flesh. Not able to see the ground, and being bone-weary, he made a rough landing on the sand.

Pat Conniry, a determined young man who used to fly at Torrance beach, decided he would fly longer than had anyone else before him. Because the lifeguards wouldn't allow hang gliding before 3 p.m., in spite of the fact that an earlier start was necessary to avoid landing in the dark, Pat had to smuggle his kite to the top of the cliff to attempt a new record. Once in the air, he was able to avoid the lifeguards, and the police, who were trying to coax him down with bullhorns. But Pat persisted; 3 hours 36 minutes after takeoff, he landed.

On August 13, Mike Mitchell topped the record with a flight of 3 hours 45 minutes at Torrey Pines, California. In order to capture the record once and for all, Bob Wills, now president of

Fig. 1-9. Rudy Kishazy soars Mont Blanc in France at 15,766 feet. (Courtesy Delta Wing Kites and Gliders, Inc.)

his own company, Sport Kites, scouted the beaches and cliffs in Hawaii. On September 1, 1973 at Waimanalo Bay, Bob and his brother Cliff took off. Cliff soon succumbed to the cold and landed. But shortly thereafter, he tied a jacket to his kite and took off again. Passing near Bob's kite, Cliff was able to drop the jacket to his brother to keep him warm. Bob stayed up for an incredible 5 hours 6 minutes while a television helicopter hovered nearby taking pictures of his flight.

Two days later, while Pat Conniry was at work just a few minutes from Torrance beach, a friend burst into his office with the news of Bob Wills' new record. Pat took his hang glider and dashed to the site. He flew over the Labor Day crowd at Buff's Cove for 5 hours 21 minutes. They toasted him as he soared overhead.

Meanwhile, the Wills family was returning from Hawaii; Cliff from his honeymoon, and Bob from his record-setting flight (or so he thought it to be). Then the news of Pat Conniry's record reached him. Bob bought a ticket for the next flight back to Hawaii, determined to fly longer than ever. On September 15, 1973 he succeeded by flying for 8 hours 24 minutes through clouds and fog, and gliding as high as 2220 feet over the takeoff point. The challenge was met.

John Hughes, who used to fly his kite over the cliffs in Hawaii, went out one day to watch a kite-company crew attempt a new record. John assembled his old kite and took off just for the fun of it; while the other fellows landed one by one, John stayed up hour after hour. He finally landed—at 11 p.m.—setting a record of 10 hours 5 minutes.

The latest word from New Zealand is that somebody has soared 25 miles to a predetermined goal, returning by air to the starting point; a flight of more than 50 miles. Just recently, somebody in Phoenix, Arizona hit a huge thermal (called a "boomer") and rose more than 5700 feet above the starting point.

Where will it end? Clearly, duration achievements are only limited by prevailing wind conditions and the determination of the pilot. Most pilots say that the true test of a kite and its pilot's ability is to soar to great heights and fly cross-country. Mike Harker passed that test when he launched his delta-wing craft from the Zugspitze in Germany on August 21, 1972. He soared for 12 minutes before landing in a snow-covered field in Austria. Most recently, on a foggy day in July 1974, he flew from Mount Fuji in Japan and landed on a mountain trail 4290 feet above sea level.

Today, the hang gliding picture is quite promising. Over 10,000 pilots belong to the United States Hang Gliding Association. Many more thousands belong to other associations, or fly alone. Peter Brock, the president of the Hang Glider Manufacturer's Association and a flier himself, reports that more than 1000 kites are sold every month in the United States. His son, 10-year-old Hall Brock, is an accomplished flier with many trophies, attesting not only to his skill but to the safety and reliability of hang gliders as well (Fig. 1-10).

Extrapolating the happenings of recent years, and combining our forecasts with the public's enthusiasm for anything new, dynamic, and exciting, it is not too difficult to envision a meteoric rise for this sport. True, there may be

Fig. 1-10. Hall Brock, champion junior kite flier.

some accidents, but no more than occur on motorcycles or skis.

Enthusiasts foresee great parks devoted to hang gliding. Already there are two commercial parks in the Los Angeles area where a variety of hills are available for instruction, contests, and advanced flying. (Unfortunately, there are no hangars for kite storage.) It's not improbable that someday skilike towing devices will pull kites and pilots back to their starting points. This development alone would entice many people who are unable to carry a 35-pond kite up a hill. A whole mountainside could be developed for hang gliding exclusively. Smooth landing sites, windsocks, and other refinements could make this sport as popular as skiing. The Grand Targhee Ski Resort in Wyoming's Tetons, about 80 miles from Idaho Falls, has already hosted hang gliding events. The day will no doubt come when weekend trains will take enthusiasts to faraway places where wind conditions will practically guarantee perfect flights. Year-around utilization of ski resorts for hang gliding is a distinct possibility. Cross-country flying will become a pleasurable pastime once air routes are worked out. Perhaps in the not too distant future, hang gliding will be an international sport or an Olympic event. Whatever happens, we can be sure one thing; the future of the sport is in the hands of safety-minded pilots, rather than reckless daredevils. The principal advantages of this sport lie in the fact that very little equipment is needed to construct a glider, and the glider pilot is able to take off without assistance. For extended flights, the future pilot will have a simple seat; hence, it can be forgiven that future pilots will not *hang* in the strictest sense.

Chapter 2

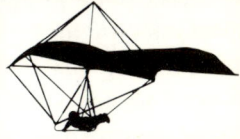

Basic Aerophysics

A really complete course on automobile driving teaches the fundamentals of internal combustion. A good course of instruction for those aspiring to be race car drivers also presents such factors as cornering force, coefficient of friction, and torque. Why must a race car driver know anything about pistons and the like, when all he has to do is "lead-foot" from start to finish? The answer is simple: the more the driver knows about the physics which influence his car, the more intelligently he will be able to drive, and the better his chances of winning. For instance, knowing that greater friction exists between a wide tire and a dry road than between a narrow tire and a wet surface, can mean the difference between crashing and winning the race. Don't think that *all* the answers are obvious, however. For many years, race cars used skinny tires; until some engineers decided to look into the basic forces involved. Their studies instigated the evolution of the wide tire. Answers are not always instinctively derived. It would be foolish to apply the brakes while rounding a curve. The car may spin out because weight has been transferred to the front, which in turn reduces cornering force in the rear—applying power in a turn actually keeps the rear end "glued" to the road, due to the natural torque reaction of the chassis (front-engine cars).

Similar considerations affect flying. Air is an invisible medium. You seldom see the effects of air flow: vortexes and turbulence. Yet these factors greatly affect the flight of an airplane. Large corporations, government agencies, and private concerns have spent large sums of money in the study of flight physics. The results of their efforts are safe airplanes which can fly even under the most adverse of conditions. Most surprising, the basic physical laws governing light-plane flight also affect hang gliders. In this chapter, I describe the most important factors which influence your flight, for understanding the laws of flight will make you think in the air—and insure your safety, as well. You will be able to analyze your mistakes and learn from the mistakes of others.

This is not a formal course in aerodynamics; the descriptions which follow (in simple language) deal with the basics only. If you wish to learn more about flight than is presented here, I suggest a more advanced book.

WHAT MAKES IT FLY?

This question, asked most often by those who see a hang glider for the first time, has a simple answer: Aircraft wings moving through air generate upward forces which, when they equal or exceed the weight of the plane and pilot, keep the plane aloft. If no air moves around the wing of the plane, the plane will not fly. The movement of air need only be relative to the movement of the wing: either the plane can be moving forward and the air still; or the plane can be still and the air moving—usually, a combination of both movements is present. The relative movement of air and wing is necessary for the generation of lift. If you'd like to test this theory, simply hold your hand out of the car window while traveling on the highway; tilting your hand upward slightly, you will feel it being lifted up. Similarly, if you park the car facing into a fairly fast wind, you will feel the same force lifting your hand. If you were to hold a surface larger than your hand, the lifting force would be greater. If you tilt the front edge of the "wing" upwards more, the lifting force will be greater, but you will also notice that another force is trying to move your hand backwards: the drag generated by the air movement around the "wing."

The basic elements affecting flight are: relative air-to-wing movement, angle of attack, air velocity, lift, and drag. The faster the air moves past the wing, the more lift generated. The larger the angle of attack, the more lift generated. The *angle of attack* (Fig. 2-1) is measured between the plane of the wing and the plane of its motion. If the path of the wind is not horizontal, the wing must be tilted correspondingly, so that the angle of attack will be true between the plane movement and that of the wing. If the angle of attack is negative (the front of the wing points downwards below the line of wing motion), the wing will be forced downwards. This *negative lift* is utilized only by control surfaces (flaps).

Lift (Fig. 2-2) is a force pointing straight upwards—at a right angle to wing movement. *Drag* is a force acting in a direction downstream of the wing. The combination of lift and drag creates another force equal to the weight of the glider. Lift and drag are forces that have magnitude (depending on velocity, surface area, etc.) and direction. Such forces are expressed mathematically as *vectors*. Often used to represent forces acting on objects, vectors can be combined into new vectors; in sailing, the wind vector and sail vector can be combined to result in a boat-movement vector. Vectors play a very important part in engineering; they make it possible to analyze the forces acting on a structure (such as a wing), and thus enable us to design structures strong enough to withstand the resultant forces.

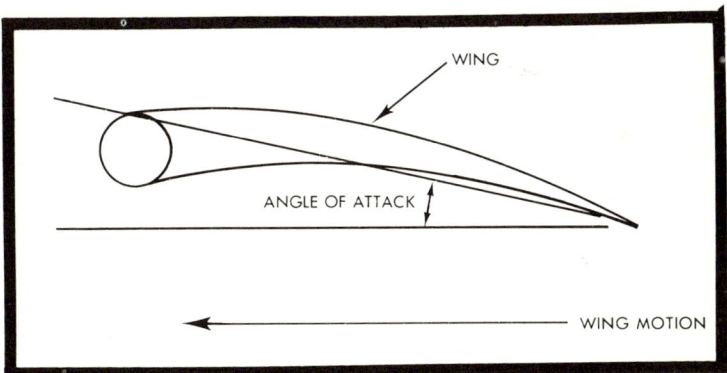

Fig. 2-1. Lift is the result of air movement relative to a curved surface and its angle of attack.

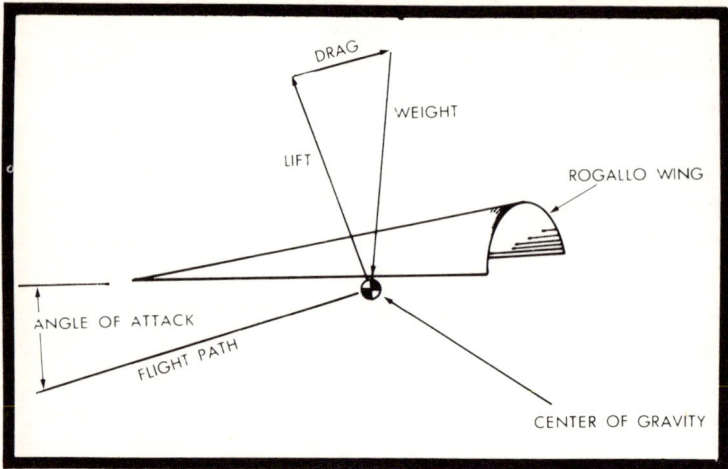

Fig. 2-2. Relationships of lift, weight, and drag.

If one force vector is opposed by another of equal magnitude but acting in the opposite direction, the result is no motion at all; if two people push with the same force on the same door from opposite sides, the door will simply not budge. If a vector is unopposed, it will move the object upon which it is acting.

The early pioneers of flight found that a surface which has curvature will experience more lift than a flat surface. Bird's wings have a decidedly curved cross section. Bird's wings also have thickness, but our ultralight hang gliders are not affected by the thickness of wing sections very much. In order to evaluate the performance of a curved wing, let us test it in an imaginary wind tunnel. Let us assume air velocity to be constant throughout the tests; and let us attach imaginary force gages to the front as well as to the bottom of the wing to measure drag and lift. The only variable will be the angle of attack. All right—start the wind machine; keep track of the forces and mark down the gage readings at every angular degree. The results will be plotted on a graph, such as the one in Fig. 2-3.

When the wing is completely parallel to its plane of motion, no lift will be generated—but there will be some drag.

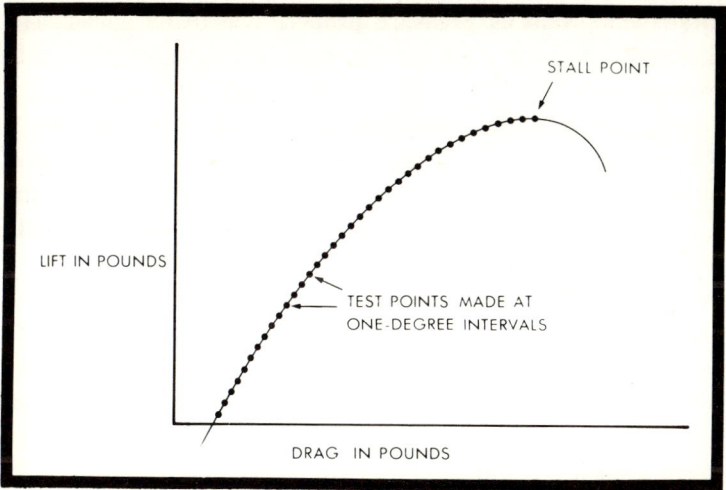

Fig. 2-3. The Lift vs drag curve.

Thus, the curve will start somewhere on the horizontal axis of the graph. At an angle of 1 degree there will be some lift, while the drag is almost the same. Plot these values on the graph; as you progress to higher angles of attack, lift will increase drastically while drag changes very little. You should be able to see that it is best to fly the wing at a slight angle, creating maximum lift with little drag. Progressively greater angles of attack soon cause only minimal lift increases while, at the same time, drag becomes quite large. At a certain angle of attack (perhaps 20 degrees or so) lift suddenly decreases while drag becomes drastically greater. This is called the *stall point*. It will be impossible for this wing to generate more lift unless its shape is changed or wind velocity is increased.

The graph obtained is called the *lift−drag curve*, or simply *L/D curve*. It will later be seen how this curve determines the flight characteristics of any airplane. The curve can be shifted slightly by varying the parameters (cross section, curvature, etc.) but basically it will remain the same.

What generates lift? A wing set at an angle causes some air to move towards its underside, creating some lifting force. Most of the lifting force, however, is generated by air rushing *over* the wing. It is a basic law of physics that a moving airstream produces pressure proportional to its speed. The airstream moving over a wing must move faster than that moving under it; it has to cover a greater distance *over* the curved area than the airstream moving *under* the wing. Thus, pressure is *lower* above the wing, causing a *relative vacuum* above the wing. The vacuum, which appears to "suck" the wing upwards, allows surrounding air pressure—now met with less resistance from above—to push the wing upwards, thus providing lifting force. Rogallo wings are slightly curved (relative to the plane of wing motion, the surface is straight) but, as was pointed out earlier, even flat surfaces generate lift when an angle of attack is introduced. If there is no angle of attack, the air pressure becomes equalized on the upper and lower sides of the wing and the hang glider ceases to fly.

Drag is caused by air turbulence acting on a wing. There are two kinds of drag: the kind caused by protrusions on the airplane, such as buckles, posts, ropes, and the pilot (drag can be reduced substantially by flying in a prone position); and the kind created by wing-produced air deflection. The net effect of both kinds is the *actual drag* used when constructing the L/D curve. The drag caused by protrusions, *parasitic drag*, increases tremendously as the speed of a hang glider increases. Drag caused by air deflection decreases slowly as flying speed goes up. (See Fig. 2-4.)

Angle of attack, airspeed, and stalling can be visualized easily if you think of water skiing. When the water skier is *in* the water, it takes a tremendous amount of power to pull him; this is due to his parasitic drag. He sets the ski at a steep angle of attack to create lift at slow speeds. Once he is *on top* of the water, little force is required to pull him; he generates little resistance and his angle of attack need not be very great. His skis are small relative to wings, and he moves at speeds relatively slow compared to airspeeds because water is so very much denser than air. (More molecules strike the ski per unit of time than strike a wing in thin air.) When forward movement stops, his skis stop lifting; he sinks.

Let us consider an important safety aspect of *stall speed*. Let us suppose that a given hang glider wing has a stall speed

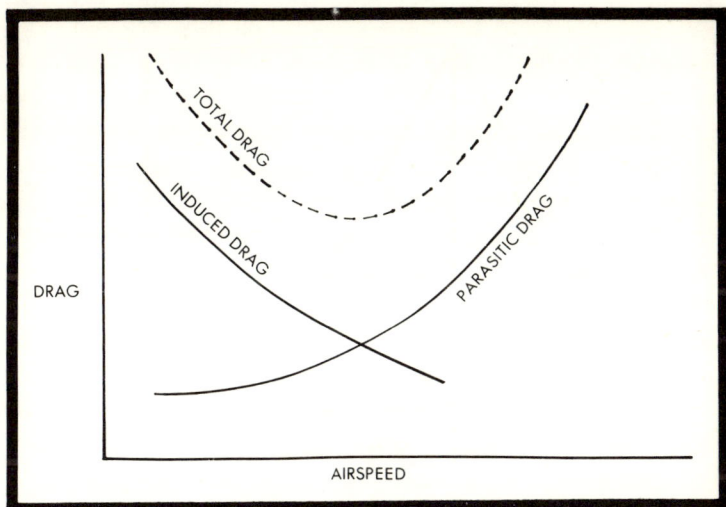

Fig. 2-4. Drag vs airspeed.

of 15 mph. Let us also suppose the glider is flying at 18 mph. All is well, until the pilot executes a tight left turn. In a tight turn the glider pivots around one of the wingtips. The other wingtip, now flying at a much higher speed, generates more lift. Thus, the outside wing raises up. The inside wingtip, flying at a much slower speed (in this case about 14 mph), loses its lift, stalls, and the plane plummets to earth; unless the pilot regains flying speed for the inside wingtip by resuming a straight course. One can easily see that a long wing may have large airspeed differentials. The short-spanned Rogallo wings have few problems in this respect.

It is important to be able to calculate the lifting surface area when planning a hang glider. For conventional straight-wing airplanes, one simply multiplies wingspan by the chord (wing width) in feet, to derive the plane area in square feet. The curvature of the surfaces is not a consideration. For a Rogallo wing the calculation is slightly different, although just as simple. The Rogallo is made of two triangles—left and right—both identical. Since the area of a triangle is equal to its base times its height divided by two, and since we have two triangles, the numerical constant can be dropped from the

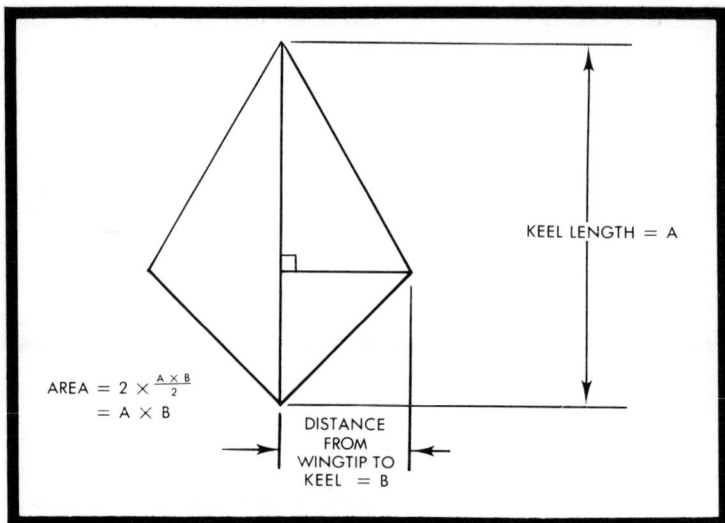

Fig. 2-5. How to calculate the surface area of a Rogallo wing.

formula, giving us: Area equals keel length times the distance between wingtip and keel. Again, the curvature of the surfaces does not have to be considered; only the plan-projection of the two triangles (Fig. 2-5).

Now let us calculate *wing loading*: the weight carried by each unit of wing area; or simply, gross weight (pilot plus glider) divided by wing area (in square feet).

Wing loading is a clue to hang glider performance. Most Rogallo wings fly best at around 1 lb/sq ft loading, especially for beginners and on calm days (Fig. 2-6). On windier days and for faster, more controlled flights, wing loadings of up to 1.5 lb/sq ft can be considered. As an example, let us consider an 18 ft, 35 lb Rogallo. Its wing area is close to 200 sq ft. Consider also a pilot weighing 165 lb. Knowing these factors, we can easily calculate gross weight to be 200 lb; and dividing this by wing area, the wing loading is 1 lb/sq ft—just about ideal for a start. You can always add more weight to a kite to compensate for windy days, or to increase its speed, but a small kite cannot be lightened easily. Low wing loadings not only result in low flying speeds (and hence lower and safer stall speeds) but also in lower sink speeds.

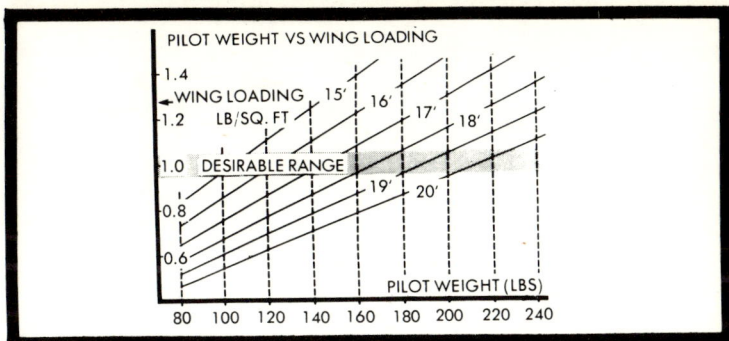

Fig. 2-6. Recommended relationship between wing size and pilot weight.

Sink speed is the rate of altitude loss, usually calculated in feet per second. Although your glider may be flying very fast, if it is flying at a shallow angle you will sink slowly. Similarly, although you may be flying slowly, if your angle is steep your sink speed will be low. To make best distance, increase flying speed. To gain soaring time, aim for a low sink speed. Low wing loading and/or high angle of attack results in low sink speeds.

Glide ratio describes the amount of altitude drop relative to the amount of forward movement (in feet). For Rogallo wings, the glide ratio is usually around 4:1, meaning that for every 4 feet of forward movement, the glider sinks 1 foot. This also means that for a sink speed of, say, 1 ft/sec, the glider will move forward relative to the ground at 4 ft/sec. Flying speed will be more than 4 ft/sec because of the relationship between ground speed and airspeed (Fig. 2-7).

To illustrate this point, let us again view velocity as a vector. Velocity, a vector quantity, has direction and magnitude (the value of which is speed). If you drew a diagram of an airplane in flight, there would be three velocity vectors acting on its motion, as shown in Fig. 2-7. One is pointed downwards: sink speed. Another, horizontal, is groundspeed. A third, slanted at the *glide angle*, represents airspeed; i.e., the speed of the airplane relative to surrounding air. If there is a headwind, groundspeed will diminish; the headwind vector acts in opposition. The actual groundspeed is

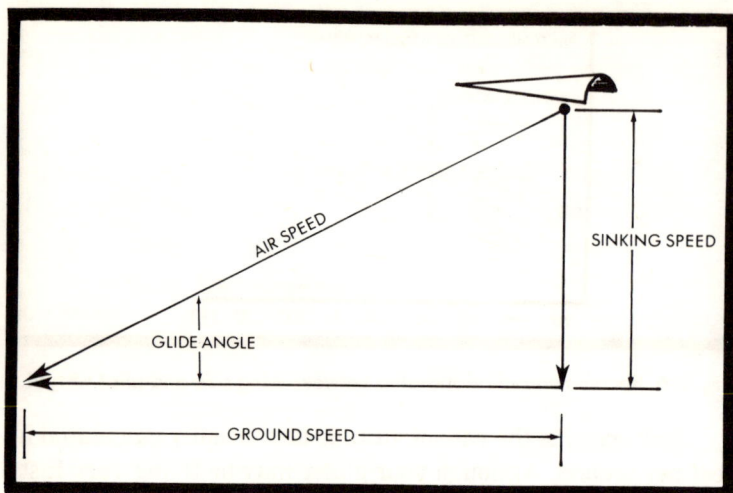

Fig. 2-7. Glide ratio equals x:y.

equivalent to the difference between groundspeed in still air and the headwind's speed. Thus, if a plane has a groundspeed (in still air) of 20 mph, and there is a 10 mph headwind, the actual groundspeed (against the wind) will be 10 mph. Note that the sink speed has not changed at all; and neither did flying speed because, after all, the airplane is only in flight as a result of its wing moving relative to the surrounding air mass. Velocity vectors will be discussed further in later paragraphs. It is only important at this point that you remember that the flight characteristics of a hang glider always depend on airspeed (i.e., speed relative to surrounding air); *not* groundspeed.

Here is a table of glide angles and their corresponding glide ratios.

Glide angle in degrees	Glide ratio
1:1	45
1:2	25
1:3	18
1:4	14
1:5	12
1:6	10

If a hang glider rises due to a *thermal* (air currents going upwards), its glide angle may be zero, or even negative; but glide angle as such is usually measured in still air. Numerically, *glide ratio* is equivalent to the cotangent of the *glide angle*, and the lift-to-drag ratio.

The *aspect ratio* of a wing is the ratio of its span (length) to its chord (width). For a straight wing this is easy to calculate. A 20-foot wing which is 4 feet wide has an aspect ratio 5:1. Rogallo wings are triangular and do not lend themselves to a simple calculation. Their aspect ratio is calculated by the formula

$$\text{aspect ratio} = \frac{\text{span}^2}{\text{wing area}}$$

Although these factors don't act coincidentally, increasing the aspect ratio provides a better glide ratio.

An object at rest on a surface is said to be in *static equilibrium*. Its weight is supported by the surface; there are no unbalancing forces acting on it to make it move in any direction. When a body is acted upon by forces while it is in motion, and that body is moving at a constant speed, it is said to be in *dynamic equilibrium*. A water skier is in dynamic equilibrium as he follows the boat. Similarly, when an airplane is in flight without undergoing violent maneuvers, it is in dynamic equilibrium.

A bicycle rider is also in dynamic equilibrium. Why doesn't his bicycle throw him to the ground? Because the forces acting on the bike are balanced around one point: the *center of gravity*. Similarly, when an airplane is flying level, the forces acting on its various parts are balanced around the center of gravity. If one of the forces becomes larger or smaller, an equal and opposite force has to be introduced to restore equilibrium; or else the center of gravity has to be shifted to a new location to restore dynamic equilibrium.

Center of gravity, or balance point, can be pictured as a pivot (like a universal joint) located somewhere within the mass of the plane-and-pilot—a point around which all forces and masses are considered balanced. One can imagine the center of gravity to be a tiny ball, within which the mass of the airplane-and-pilot is concentrated. The center of gravity follows a *true* flight path; the other parts of the plane follow slightly different paths. The outboard wingtip, for example, describes a greater arc than the inner wingtip in a turn; the center of gravity describes a true circular path somewhere in between.

All movements of the airplane can be considered to be around the center of gravity as if it were a gimbal. There are three imaginary axes around which movement can take place. The *vertical axis* goes through the center of gravity; *yaw*, or turning, takes place around this axis. The *roll axis* is generally aligned longitudinally with the plane; in a Rogallo wing this roughly coincides with the keel. The plane *rolls* (dips its wings or "banks") around this axis. The *pitch axis* goes through the center of gravity laterally. As the nose of the plane goes up and down, the plane is said to be *pitching* (Fig. 2-8).

In order to highlight some of these principles, try to picture a jet plane taking off. Its center of gravity describes a smooth, curving path. Just before its wheels leave the ground, you can observe it lift its nose: it rotates around the pitch axis.

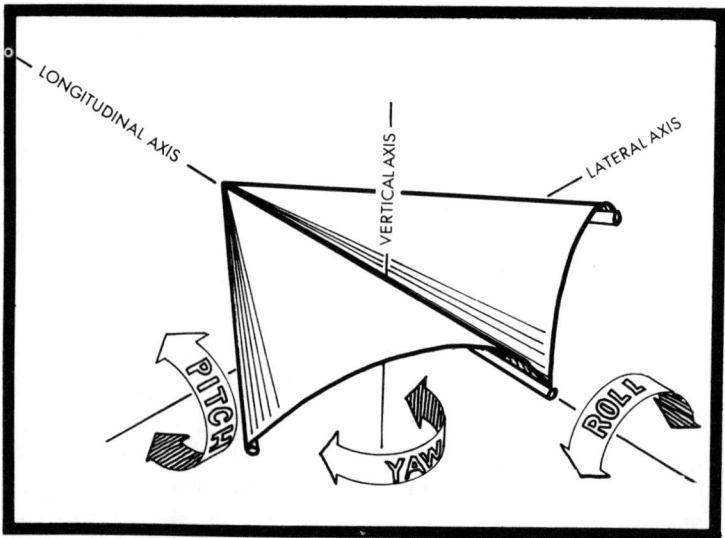

Fig. 2-8. The three axes of plane movement. (Courtesy Whitney Enterprises)

It may dip its wings as a result of wind gusts (i.e., rotate around the roll axis), but the center of gravity still moves in a smooth path.

In a regular airplane and in advanced fixed-wing gliders there may be as many as three controls to affect rotation around these axes. The control surfaces attached to the trailing edges of the wings, *ailerons*, control movement around the roll axis. The *rudder* controls movement around the yaw axis. The *elevator* lifts or dips the tail to rotate the plane around the pitch axis. In a basic hand glider, axis control is achieved by the pilot shifting his weight; he changes the position of the center of gravity.

Whereas lift can be thought of as the action of tiny little fingers holding up a wing, it can also be thought of as a gigantic hand acting on one point only: the center of lift, or *center of pressure*. If the center of pressure coincides with the center of gravity, the plane is balanced and will fly straight; if lift acts in front of the center of gravity, it will nose-up. If left unchecked, a nose-up attitude will cause the plane to stall because the angle of attack is increased. If the center of pressure is behind the center of gravity (when the pilot shifts his weight forward), the front of the plane will pitch down; the plane would go into a dive if unchecked. Similarly, if the pilot shifts his weight left of the center of pressure, the plane will bank (roll) to the left. These movements are caused by force couples, or *moments*. A moment of force, like torque, is the product of a force and its distance from a pivot point. Although two torques may be equal in value, the forces or distances involved may be different. For instance, you may have a very powerful, air-driven torque wrench which can take the nuts off a car's wheels; but with a moment arm long enough (long wrench), a child could do the same job without all that power.

The unit of moments (or torque) is the foot-pound. Let me explain with this example: A 200 lb man who puts his entire weight on a foot-long torque wrench to remove a rusty nut exerts 200 ft-lb of torque. The screw holding the rusty nut may have a diameter of 2 inches. In this case, the radius upon which the torque acts is 1 inch. The force acting tangentially at this point is exactly balanced by the undoing torque the moment the nut comes loose. Thus, a 200 ft-lb torque must equal a distance of 1 inch ($^1/_{12}$ ft) times some force. Mathematically, it looks like this:

$$200 \times 1 = {^1/_{12}} \times \text{unknown force.}$$

This can be calculated by algebra and is found to be 2400 pounds of force! These calculations may sound like so much gobbledegook, but consider their effect; to balance an airplane statically (before it leaves the ground), all moments attributed to the various components must be exactly balanced around the center of gravity. Consider a fixed-wing plane. Suppose the pilot weighs 180 pounds and he hangs from a hook located 1 foot ahead of the center of gravity; the result would be a moment acting in one direction with a magnitude of 180 times 1 foot: 180 ft-lb. This force has to be balanced perfectly by the moment generated by the tail. If the tail weighs 18 lb, its center-of-mass must be located exactly 10 ft behind the center of gravity; resulting in 180 ft-lb of moment to balance the moment of the pilot (Fig. 2-9). If the tail were heavier, its distance from the center of gravity would have to be shortened—and vice versa. To keep wing loading down, the pilot-plus-glider weight has to be kept low. This means that the tail section must be very light so the *tail moment* is low; to balance it, the pilot must be positioned very close to, and in front of, the center of gravity. This is the reason ultralight, fixed-wing hang gliders seem to be very short: the pilot's weight does not have to balance a

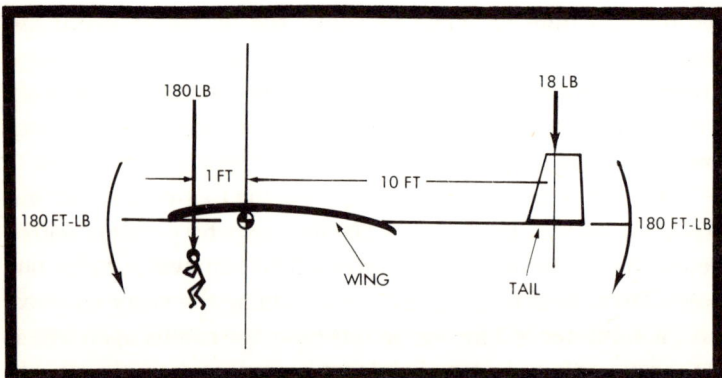

Fig. 2-9. The theory of moments applied to a fixed-wing airplane.

heavy tail section. In larger powered planes, engine weight has to be balanced by a long or heavy tail.

Moment theory comes into important play during turns. The Rogallo wing has a very short span; as a result, the center of pressure of each wing is very close to the keel (roll axis)—and in the lateral direction, may be located only 3 feet from it. The lifting-force-times-distance (3 ft) can be easily counteracted by a 180 lb pilot shifting his weight 1 ft to the side. On a long-winged airplane, the center of pressure may be located 6 ft from the pilot. He would have to shift his weight at least 2 ft to that side to produce a counteracting effect. A 2 ft shift takes a lot of strength and time; it does not lend itself to precise control. Hence, long-winged gliders are equipped with ailerons which control roll by utilizing aerodynamic forces.

Hang glider pilots have their weight concentrated far below the wing. This results in a pendulum effect. Just as a pendulum tends to return to rest, so does a hang glider pilot when upset by a gust of wind. Stability is inherent.

The maneuverability of a hang glider depends greatly on its moment of inertia. This is a rather complex phenomenon which can be explained by referring to an analogy with a barbell. A barbell suspended from a string would take quite a bit of force before it would start to spin. It would also take quite a bit of force to stop it. If the weights were placed on a much longer bar, it would be even harder to start it spinning, or to stop it. This is because when the weights are placed far from the center, their moment of inertia is large. When the same weights are placed close to the center, it is easy to stop the barbell from spinning. In fact, the more concentrated the weights—i.e., placed closer to the center of rotation—the more maneuverable they will be. Applying this principle to a hang glider, it should be apparent that wingtips which are heavy, or located far from the center of gravity, will not only make it difficult to turn, but will also make it hard to stop a turn or make corrections. For this reason, wingtips and tail surfaces must be very light.

Hang gliders must be light so that their wing surfaces do not have to be very large to keep wing loading within desirable limits. Due to safety considerations, a hang glider also has to be very strong. There are ways by which these structural criteria can be satisfied. Special aircraft materials must be used; and the materials must be made in a configuration which will result in structural strength.

The study of materials and how they behave when forces are applied to them is a science. In order to acquaint the hang glider builder and user with the essential elements of this subject, only the most important basics will be discussed. The reader is referred to standard engineering texts for an in-depth discussion.

When a force is applied to a part, the force is spread more or less evenly across the cross section of that part. Each unit of area supports part of the force. Force-per-unit-area, called *stress*, can be *compressive*, as when a column supports the weight of a roof, or it can be *tensile*, as when a rope supports a weight. It can also be a *torsional*, as found in the drive shafts of cars; but this kind seldom applies to hang gliders. The force of stress is usually measured in pounds; the area experiencing the force is measured in square inches:

$$\text{stress} = \frac{\text{force (lb)}}{\text{area (sq in.)}}$$

Thus, stress is expressed in pounds per square inch, or psi.

All materials are somewhat elastic. When a force is applied to them, they either stretch (elongate), compress (or bend), or twist. The deformation produced by stress is called *strain*. Stress and strain are usually confused by nonexperts. Stress is the cause; strain, the effect.

To visualize these principles, picture a spring, the end of which is attached to a weight—either in tension (as in a fish-scale), or compression (as on a conventional scale).

When we place a weight (force) on the spring, stress is applied to it. The spring either stretches or compresses; the deformation is strain. The strain on a spring is large; the strain in structural members is usually quite small—although measurable by precision instruments.

Now let us turn our attention to a wood beam placed between two supports and holding a weight at its center. The beam will curve downwards (Fig. 2-10). The action of the wood

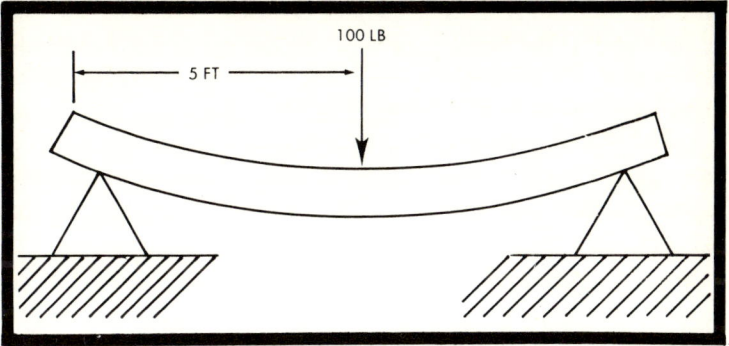

Fig. 2-10. Concentrated load on a beam.

fibers can be visualized if we place a hinge in the center, a coil spring between the butted ends above the hinge, and a coil spring below the hinge. When the load is applied, the spring above the hinge compresses as the spring below the hinge stretches. It can also be demonstrated that the same kind of action that occurs in wood fibers also occurs between metal molecules when a load is applied to a long span in a crosswise direction. If the direction of the load is reversed, tension and compression will simply interchange (Fig. 2-11).

Now, let us recall the theory of moments. I stated that to have equilibrium, moments acting in opposition must be equal. This principle can be applied to a simple beam 2 inches thick

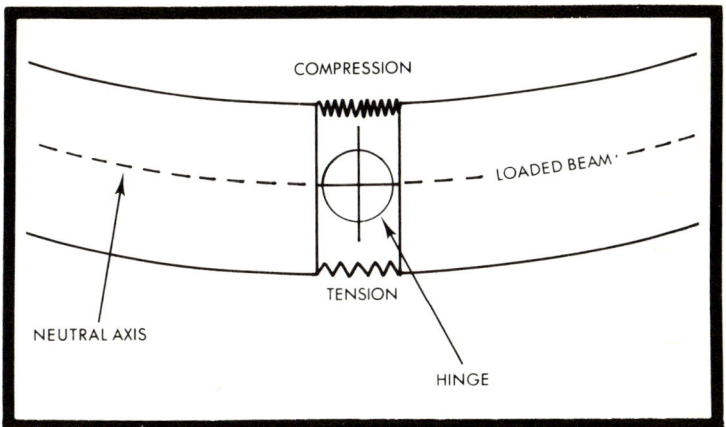

Fig. 2-11. Tension and compression in a beam.

(e.g., an aluminum tube in a kite) and 10 feet long, we have the following considerations suspended between two supports, one at each end. If the load applied, is 100 pounds, acting exactly in the middle, the bending moment would be equal to force times distance: 100 lb $\times$ 5 ft = 500 ft-lb. This moment has to be balanced, or counteracted, by the strength of the material. If we consider the imaginary hinge to be located in the center of the beam, the *neutral axis* (neither tension nor compression occurs there), only pure rotation around the hinge pin occurs and the tension force on the lower surface of the beam will have to be equal to 500 ft-lb. The moment arm at the lower surface (i.e., the distance from the hinge pin to the surface) is 1 inch, or $^1/_{12}$ ft. The moment, equal to $^1/_{12}$ ft times tension force, is 500 ft-lb. The calculated tension force will be found to be approximately 6000 lb. If the cross section of the beam at that point is 1 sq in., the stress will be 6000 lb/sq in. (in tension). Similarly, the compressive stress can be found. All materials are stronger in compression than in tension and, for this reason, only the tensile stresses are calculated. (Care must be taken to prevent compressive buckling.) Remember that unit loading in a beam can be reduced if the load is distributed uniformly.

All available engineering materials have been tested in scientific laboratories; the results are published in tables. Knowing the exact stress at each point and the size of the structural member, one merely selects the suitable material—the lightest available that can withstand the stress.

Most materials behave like a spring when they are subjected to a tensile load. They will stretch to a certain degree. If the load doubles, the material will doubly stretch. There comes a point, however, when the material stretches more than proportionally. Although the material may be still in one piece, and not break until an even higher force is applied (the *ultimate strength*), designers never exceed the proportional limit of stretch. As an example, the average proportional limit of steel is 40,000 psi, and that of aluminum is 8000 psi. Steel, weighing 2.8 times as much as aluminum, is five times stronger. Weight-for-weight, steel is thus stronger than aluminum. Aluminum is used because of its workability and low price compared to steel.

It would be unwise to calculate exactly the stress in a material, and then use the material in a size matching the stress exactly; sudden wind gusts, or landing shock, can result in unexpectedly high loadings. The design stress is doubled for large airplanes where loads are fairly predictable; for modern hang gliders, the design stress is tripled. The ratio of design stress to actual stress is called the *safety factor*. After calculating the exact stress of a structural member, choose a material which at least meets triple that value. Since stress equals force-per-area, the stress level for a given force can be reduced by increasing structural area.

Engineering tables of strengths of various materials apply only to smooth, uniform members. Any structural discontinuity in a member reduces its cross-sectional area and causes stress levels to rise drastically, weakening the material dramatically. If you wanted to break off the end of a piece of wood, you would simply whittle a notch around it, making it break easily and predictably. Similarly, all breaks occur where there is *stress raiser* in the material.

If a discontinuity *must* be placed in the material, it must be done in such a manner that the change is neither sudden nor channeled in a direction which produces a stress raiser. If two materials are welded together, a stress raiser exists at the joint of cross sections. It would be best to flare (or taper) the

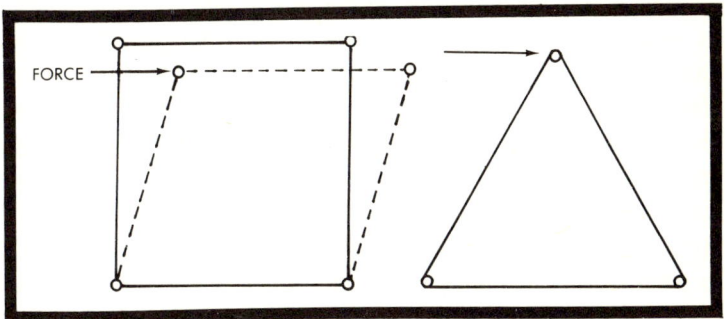

FORCE

Fig. 2-12. A square structure distorts easily when a force is applied to one of its corners; a triangle does not.

joint as much as possible. If a hole must be drilled through aluminum tubing, drill it perpendicularly to the neutral axis of bending to lessen weakening. Reputable manufacturers of kites, using this rationale, put extra sleeves on aluminum tubes at every point where a steel cable or fitting is attached. Stresses are highest at these places; the sleeve reduces stress levels to a safe value.

Cross holes drilled in square bars increase the theoretical stress value, depending on the ratio of hole diameter (d) and bar thickness (w):

Ratio of $d:w$	Stress increase
0.1	2.68
0.2	2.50
0.3	2.37
0.4	2.25
0.5	2.18
0.6	2.12
0.7	2.08
0.8	2.06

This table illustrates that if the hole is quite small compared to the thickness of the bar, the actual stress in the bar may be almost three times higher than that in a solid bar. Notches, sudden changes in cross-sectional shape, and other discontinuities in a bar or tube also increase the stress levels. In such cases, the structural part has to be larger in cross-sectional area to reduce stress to a safe value.

The strongest and simplest structural form is the triangle; its shape cannot be deformed. If a rectangular parallelogram has force applied to one of its corners, it will distort to a slanted shape (Fig. 2-12). A triangle will always retain its shape unless the strength of its material is overcome. Complex structures can be made very strong by adding triangulated stiffeners, bracing (guy) wires, or gussets. As in any complex structure, some of the members in an airframe are subjected to compressive loadings while others are in tension. Those in compression must be large in cross section to prevent buckling. A large cross section insures strength and allows the use of even weak materials. Most materials are very strong when subjected to tension, so thin sections are usually sufficient to withstand the associated stresses.

It should be obvious by now that the use of engineering and mathematics is required to produce a hang glider which is light, strong, and maximizes air currents and a pilot's ability. Before you consider modifying the airframe on your glider, consider the effect on the structure—and your life.

Chapter 3

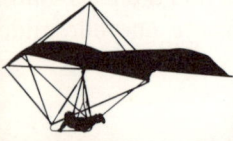

Materials and Construction

It is not the aim of this chapter to explain how to build a particular hang glider; nor to give you dimensions or construction instructions. There are several good kits available that supply these. The purpose here is to offer a comprehensive rundown of the variety of materials presently used. Although most early hang gliding kites were homemade, today the typical newcomer can write for catalogs of finished models and choose from a large number of designs which will fit him, his needs, and his pocketbook. Mass production has reduced the cost of kites to the point where it is hardly worth fooling around with your own construction—your time investment would be tremendous, and every part would have to be purchased from a specialist. You may have to drive for hours just to pick up an aircraft-quality eyebolt or to find a competent sailmaker.

Designing your own kite is not as easy as it might seem. A well designed kite uses parts chosen for strength and lightness. Using your own rules of thumb, you may come up with a part which is too weak or too heavy. For your first kite, start out with a professionally proved design that uses dimensions and proportions derived by painstaking research.

Why then are we discussing materials? The reason is simple. If you know what is available, what is reliable, and what is safe, you will be able to make an intelligent choice of kites.

Let's start with the most important part of a kite: the wing-covering material. In the early days of hang gliding, the

Fig. 3-1. A homemade plastic-covered kite takes off.

aim of the pioneers was to construct kites for the lowest possible cost in the shortest possible time (Fig. 3-1). Today, if you had to cover a large area with a cheap yet strong material, polyethylene plastic would be the best choice. You are well familiar with the plastic coverings that are used on dry cleaners' bags and outdoor equipment. This semitransparent plastic sheeting, made in many different thicknesses, is relatively strong, light, and inexpensive. It has two faults, however: Once it starts to rip, it doesn't stop by itself; and it stretches.

When you measure plastic sheeting for a hang glider, do so when the material is at room temperature. Cold plastic becomes brittle and develops tiny cracks that may eventually start long tears. Use light-colored plastic. Dark colors (especially black) absorb a lot of heat from the sun. Hot plastics stretch easily and may lose their shape. The wing must not have any wrinkles in it; wrinkles will detract from performance (Fig. 3-2). If you equip your kite with Dacron sails (after having used sheet plastic) you will find a noticeable improvement in its performance.

Sheet plastic should be reinforced with adhesive tape, such as the silver type used by plumbers on air-conditioning ducts.

Fig. 3-2. An improperly made sail loses its shape in the air.

This also applies to attaching plastic to the spars. Fasten the edge of the plastic to the spar (leading edge) at every 6 inches or so with a little tape. Next, roll the top of the spar outwards (away from the keel) so the plastic wraps around it. Finally, apply tape along the entire length of the spar to lock the tape in place. When making a Rogallo wing, this is done before the leading edges are attached to the nose plate. With both edges of the plastic taped, lay the center keel on top of the sheet and bring the sheet up on both sides of the keel. The plastic should come up to the centerline of the keel and close on top. Secure the plastic edges together with a liberal application of tape.

Modern hang gliders are covered with manmade plastic-derived fabric that provides better resistance to mildew and rot than can be afforded by cotton or wool. The best known manmade yarns are nylon and Dacron. Dacron is the more popular type for sails. The "rip-stop" process makes Dacron rip-proof. The cloth is classified according to its weight per square yard. Three-ounce cloth is inexpensive (about $1.50 per yard), but slightly porous; it is used in the cheaper kits. Better cloth is available that is less porous and is heat-stabilized, weighs about 3.8 oz/sq yd and costs over $2 per yard, wholesale.

After the cloth is measured to the proper size and cut with a hot knife to eliminate frayed edges, double-backed tape

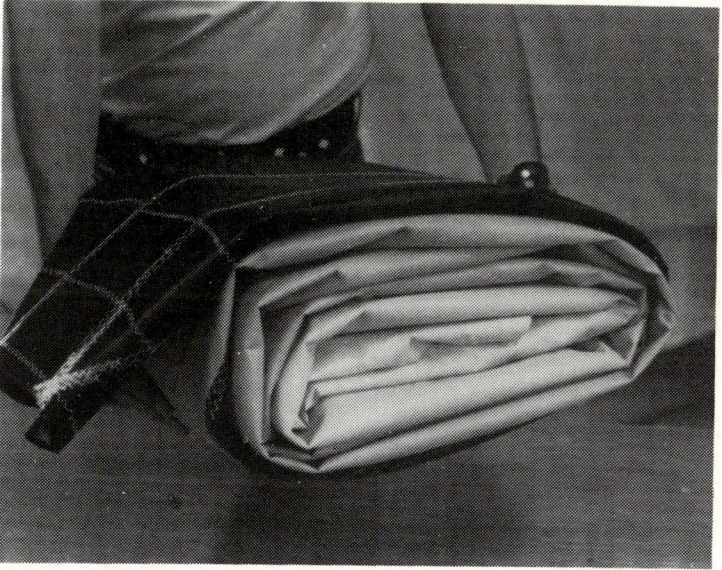

Fig. 3-3. The proper method of storing a Dacron sail. Note the zig-zag stitch.

(sticky on both sides) is applied between the panels to keep them from shifting during sewing; V-69 Dacron thread is usually used to machine-sew the cloth. The sewing machine must be of the heavy-duty type to handle the large stitching required. A zig-zag stitch should be used to comply with best sailmaking practice. Straight stitching tends to stretch and lose strength when tension is applied in flight. Zig-zag stitching, on the other hand, stretches *with* the cloth, resulting in uniform loading (Fig. 3-3). The stitch does not have to be overly strong to support the average load on it; however, local stresses do occur, especially when the spars flex during wind gusts, and may exceed normal stresses by a large margin. Grommets may be attached to the corners of the sail so that it can be attached to the ends of the tubes. While some cloth sails are taped on the leading edges—much like the plastic sails—the modern technique is to sew a sleeve at the edges of the cloth; the tubes are simply inserted in the sleeve (Fig 3-4). (This is similar to wing-masted boat sail construction.) The resulting seam makes the sail streamlined for good flight characteristics.

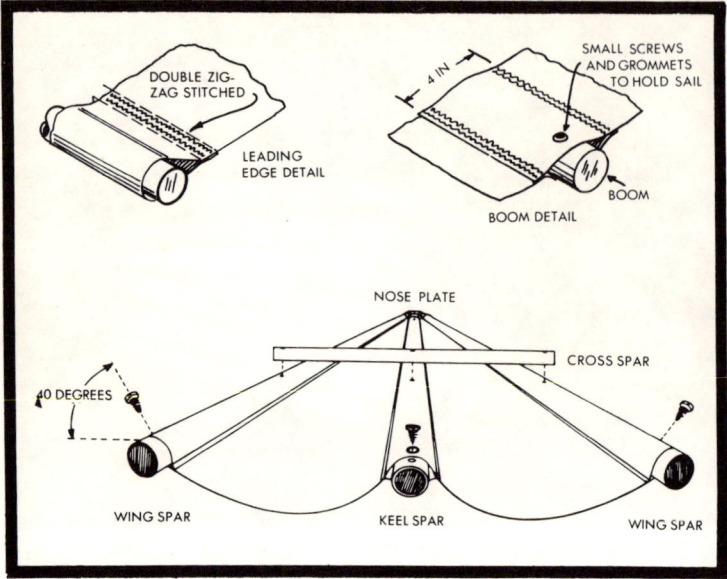

Fig. 3-4. Details of sail attachment to the spars. (Courtesy Whitney Enterprises)

Metal conduits were used originally, but these proved to be to heavy and too weak. Modern hang gliders use aluminum tubes almost exclusively.

Even though Dacron sails are almost impervious to moisture, it is best to dry them as soon as possible after a rain to prevent mildew damage. In general, the sail should be inspected every 6 months. If it had to be dismantled from the kite, it should be handled gently and stored in a cool, dry place.

Some kite fliers have *battens* installed at the trailing edge of the sail. Battens are thin strips of wood or fiberglass that are tucked into pockets at the rear edge of the sail to prevent it from fluttering. Most kite fliers, however, feel that battens contribute little to flight performances.

Other major kite components are the keel spar, the wing spars, and the cross spar (Fig. 3-5). These used to be bamboo poles when the sport was still in its infancy. Bamboo poles are light (hollow) and strong, but they have some disadvantages. The knots make it difficult to create a smooth sail; it is difficult to specify exact quality and size; and one end is always thinner than the other. For these reasons, kite fliers began to look for other materials for hang glider construction.

A rod is much heavier than a tube, and is not as strong; where can one find tubes that would be suitable for a kite?

The outstanding characteristics of aluminum are its strength-to-weight ratio, its corrosion resistance, and the fact that it can be alloyed with other metals to achieve desirable properties. The density of aluminum is about 0.1 lb/cu in.; steel has a density of 0.28 lb/cu in. Pure aluminum has a tensile strength of 8000 psi, but alloying (as well as cold-working) increases this strength substantially; and aluminum is about one-third as stiff as steel.

The corrosion resistance of aluminum can be improved by immersing it, as an anode, in an acid bath through which an electric current is passed. This process, *anodizing*, builds up a heavy layer of oxide that protects against exposure to the elements. Coatings of various colors can be applied, depending on the acid used. Aluminum and its alloys are designated by a four-digit system:

pure aluminum	1xxx
copper alloy	2xxx
manganese alloy	3xxx

Fig. 3-5. The basic elements of a flexible-wing hang glider.

silicon alloy	4xxx
magnesium alloy	5xxx
magnesium—silicon alloy	6xxx
zinc alloy	7xxx

The temper (toughness) designation, a capital letter separated from the alloy number by a hyphen, is sometimes followed by a number to designate the exact process:

| —F | as fabricated | —H | strain hardened |
| —O | annealed | —T | treated |

Number 4032-T6 is a wrought, silicon—aluminum alloy which has been solution-treated then artificially aged; 2024, the strongest, is also the most expensive aluminum tubing available; 2024-T3 is an excellent material for control bars; 6061-T6 is very popular for booms and spars; 6063-T832 is just as strong, but has more flex resistance, anodizes better, and affords easily controlled wall thickness; the tensile strength of 6061-T6 is close to 40,000 psi. Modern hang gliders use approximately 1½ in. tubing with a 0.049 to 0.058 in. wall; 10 ft pieces weigh 2.63 lb and 3.0 lb, respectively. Thus, increased wall thickness is accompanied by only a slight increase in weight. The safety offered is well worth the increased cost.

In general, one thinks of tubing as having a circular cross section with a wall thickness around $1/16$ inch. Thick-walled tubing is really pipe; pipe is heavy, has a rough outside surface, and is not usually used in hang gliders. There are pipe *fittings*, however—joints, swivels, and tees—which can be used to connect tubes. Aluminum also comes in extruded U-shapes, L-shapes, and strips, which can be used to make a variety of fittings.

At areas of added stress, or where tube strength is reduced by holes, the tubing has to be reinforced by one of three methods: an internal sleeve can be added; a wooden plug can be inserted; or an external sleeve can be put on the tube. In the latter case, the outside tube should fit snugly to the inside tube. One sheetmetal screw usually suffices to fasten the two tubes together. Tubing can be spliced together by using outside sleeves at the joints.

Wherever a bolt passes through the tube, a local stress is created which has to be distributed over a large area. Additionally, a bushing has to be installed in the hole so that the repeated assembly routine and the movement of the bolt in the tube does not wear the hole oversize and further weaken the part.

Now the main kite members are covered by the sail. How do we fasten them together? Nuts and bolts. But not the ordinary hardware-store types.

Government agencies have standardized the best (light, yet strong) fasteners in rigid military specifications. These are available for every type of nut and bolt; they also include cements, webbing, coatings, and every other material or process used by the military. These specifications, used by the aircraft industry, are also used by reputable hang glider manufacturers. Anybody can order these specifications from: Commanding Officer, Naval Publications and Forms Center, 5801 Tabor Ave., Philadelphia, PA 19120. There is a large selection of hex-head bolts, eyebolts, pulleys, locknuts, screws, pins, and other fasteners (Fig. 3-6) available from supply houses which cater to aircraft manufacturers; look them up under FASTENERS in the yellow pages. Hex-head bolts have basic characteristics signified by a code stamped on the head (Fig. 3-7).

Screw and bolt threads are designated by the outside diameter of the threaded part and the number of threads per inch: ¼ 20 means ¼ inch diameter with 20 threads per inch; ¼ 28, 28 threads per inch. Higher numbers, indicating finer threads, allow more torque to be applied. Because hang gliders are usually made from aluminum, it is best to use coursely threaded parts; they have more "body" to grip the nut.

There are two preferred methods to prevent nuts from coming loose. One is to use locknuts. A plastic insert in the nut prevents it from vibrating loose. The other method uses a safety wire. A tiny hole is drilled across the body of the bolt, and the nut has slots in it. One of the slots is aligned with the hole and a soft wire is passed through it. Loosening torque due

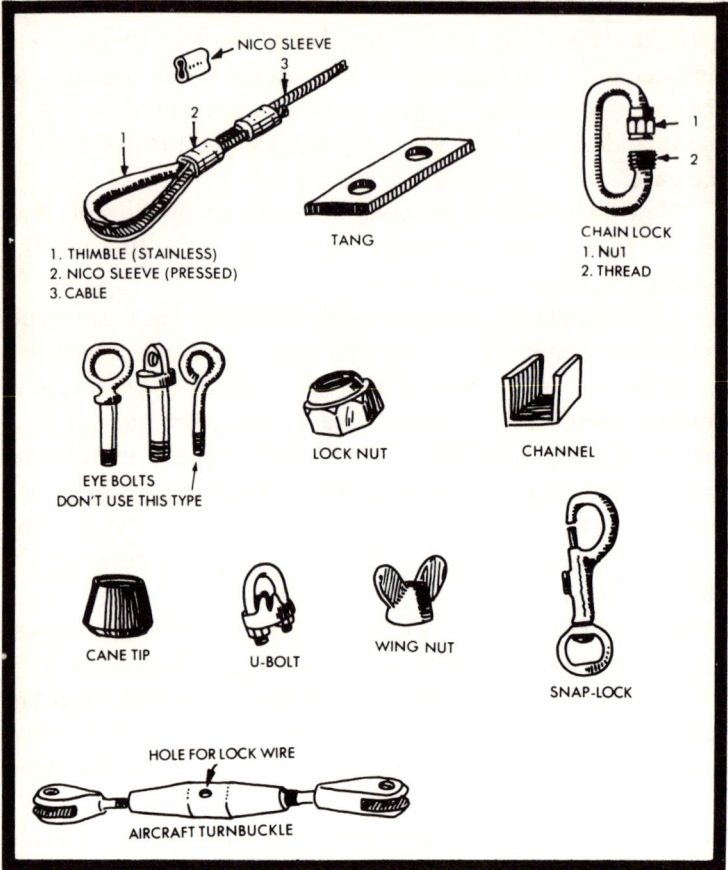

Fig. 3-6. Some fasteners used in the construction of hang gliders. (Courtesy Whitney Enterprises)

to vibration is insufficient to shear the safety wire. A washer must be used under each nut and other rotating parts. This is necessary to prevent the nut from digging into the soft aluminum and weakening it.

Eyebolts provide a convenient means of anchoring a cable to a tube. Use one-piece eyebolts—they have excellent strength throughout. Avoid the cheap bent-head, hardware-store eyebolts made from soft material. They straighten during stress applications. U-bolts can also be used to fasten two parts together.

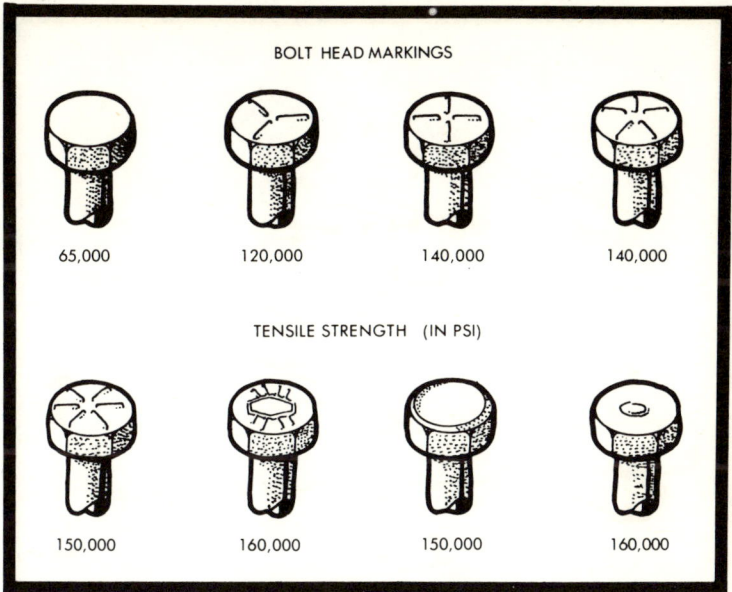

BOLT HEAD MARKINGS

65,000	120,000	140,000	140,000

TENSILE STRENGTH (IN PSI)

150,000	160,000	150,000	160,000

Fig. 3-7. Aircraft bolt head markings. (Courtesy Whitney Enterprises)

It is convenient to arrange the parts of the kite so they can be securely fastened together for flight, yet be disassembled without the use of tools. The most popular method is to use a *pip* pin (Fig. 3-8). This is a strong pin with a spring inside which presses two small balls outwards. The pin is inserted through holes in the parts to be joined; the balls extend to prevent the pin from falling out. By pressing a button or pulling a ring at the end of the pin, the inside spring is released, and the two balls retract. Less stressed pins can be secured with cotter pins or steel safety pins (Fig. 3-9).

The aluminum tubes in hang gliders do not possess sufficient strength by themselves to withstand the flying and landing loads. For this reason, all Rogallo glider parts (with the exception of the wingtips) and most parts of fixed-wing gliders are rigged together with cables. The wires located under the wings are called *flying wires* because they resist stresses in flight. The wires on top of the wings are called *landing wires* or *ground wires*; they support the structural parts when the glider is on the ground. Steel cables are used on

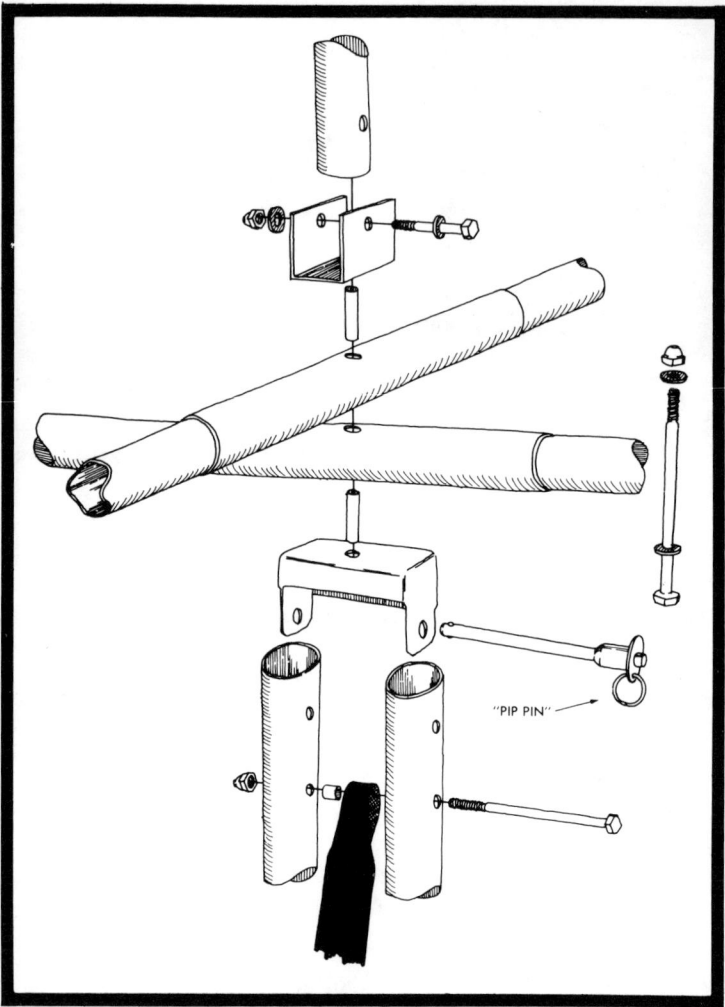

Fig. 3-8. A "pip pin" may be used to assemble the trapeze bar to the main frame. (Courtesy Chandelle Skysails)

all modern gliders. The inexpensive rigging wires used on early models stretched and broke—at inopportune times.

Steel cable is made up of many elements. Each of these consists of one central wire and six outside wires: a total of seven wires. Seven of these clusters are wound together to form the actual cable. Thus, most cables are designated 7×7. A 7×7 cable less than eighth-inch in diameter has a tensile

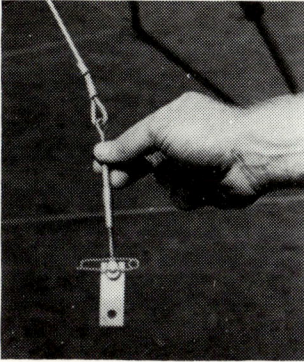

Fig. 3-9. A turnbuckle attached to a tang with a safety pin.

strength of 920 pounds; under this load it only elongates 0.001 in./ft or less. Larger, more critical areas may be rigged with a 7 × 19 cable (⅛ in. diameter) to provide the strength to take 1760 pounds in tension (Fig. 3-10).

It is necessary that the cable's point of attachment be as strong as the cable itself. Otherwise, a weak link will result in

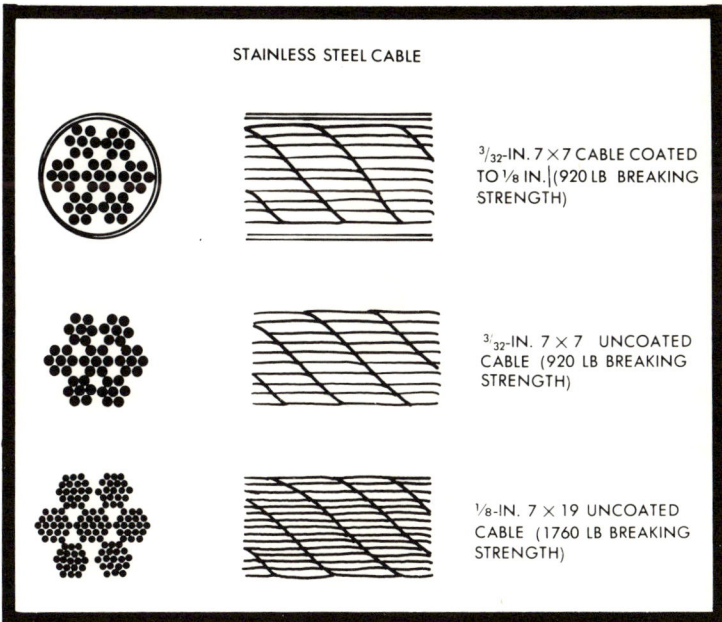

STAINLESS STEEL CABLE

³/₃₂-IN. 7 × 7 CABLE COATED TO ⅛ IN.|(920 LB BREAKING STRENGTH)

³/₃₂-IN. 7 × 7 UNCOATED CABLE (920 LB BREAKING STRENGTH)

⅛-IN. 7 × 19 UNCOATED CABLE (1760 LB BREAKING STRENGTH)

Fig. 3-10. Typical cable construction for aircraft use. (Courtesy Skycraft, Inc.)

the structural "chain." It has been found that if the cable is curled back against itself in a gentle arc and fastened in this position, its tensile strength will not be altered significantly. The arc must be held around a "thimble" (Fig. 3-6). The cable is fastened against itself by means of copper sleeves, crimped tightly with a Nicopress. This arrangement, when attached to an eyebolt, takes tension optimally; all of its loading is aligned with its axis. (Further details can be found in the chapter on tools.)

Cables are slack during the installation of associated hardware (eyebolts, pins, etc.). After nuts are tightened, cables have to be tightened also; *turnbuckles* are used for this. A turnbuckle is made in three parts: an eyebolt with a right-hand thread, an eyebolt with a left-hand thread, and a center piece with two female threads. Rotating the center piece causes the eyebolts to thread toward each other or move farther apart. Once the cables have reached the desired tightness, soft safety wire or safety pins can be used to lock the center piece in place.

The cables near the pilot should be plastic-coated to prevent wire burns (similar to rope burns) during tough landings.

There are many places on a kite where aluminum tubes must cross each other. At these points, care must be taken to avoid having the tubes flatten out while they are being tightened against each other. Modern gliders use molded plastic "cradles," in which half-round cutouts are located opposite each other in a plastic piece that is oriented at an angle to accept the crossed tubes.

The front ends of the wing spars are fastened to the keel spar (on Rogallo gliders) with a *nose plate*. This can be a single plate, two identical plates, or a plate bent almost against itself to create a space for the tubes. Bolts, located in bushings, hold the assembly together. The ends of the tubes should be capped with wooden plugs (shaped conically), plastic caps, rubber cane tips, or metal caps (Fig. 3-11).

The basic structural elements of fixed-wing gliders are essentially the same as those of flexible-wing types. The arrangement of the parts is quite different, however; the

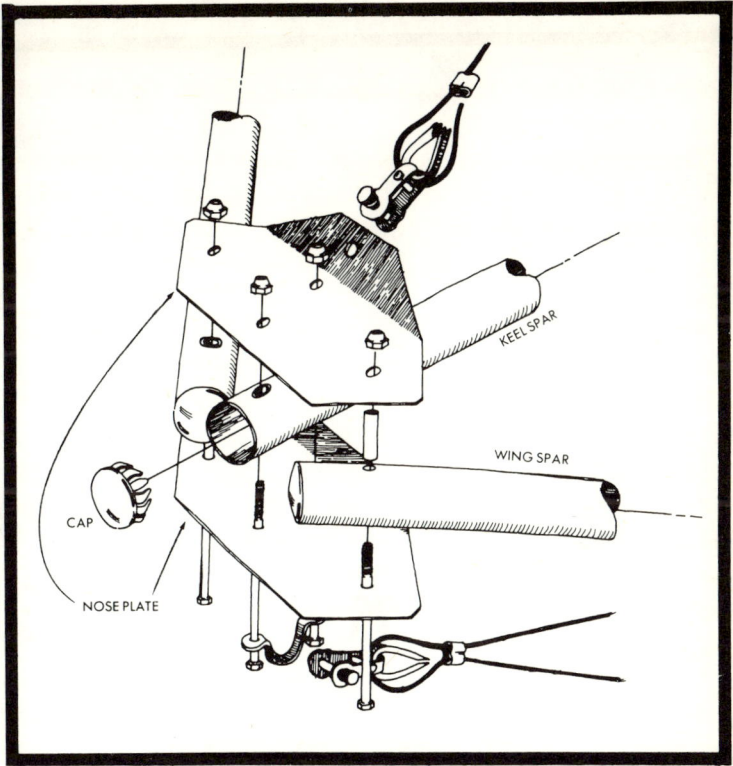

Fig. 3-11. Typical nose-plate assembly. (Courtesy Chandelle Skysails)

shape is dictated by different requirements (Fig. 3-12). The more complex fixed-wing gliders employ regular light-aircraft wood-and-doped-canvas construction (Fig. 3-13).

Sometimes a built-up wing spar with an I-beam or *box* cross section is employed as the best compromise between weight and strength. Most of the mass of wooden spars is concentrated near the surface of the wings, resulting in the highest *moment of inertia*—and the strongest structure. The ribs, built up individually from slender pieces of wood(pine or hickory), are bent to shape and glued together. Plywood gussets at the joints provide better stress distribution. The ribs are made in a jig to insure absolute uniformity and a warp-free wing. Subsequently, the ribs are fastened to the main spar. The front (curved) part of the wing is sometimes covered with veneer or thin plywood to obtain an even and true curved

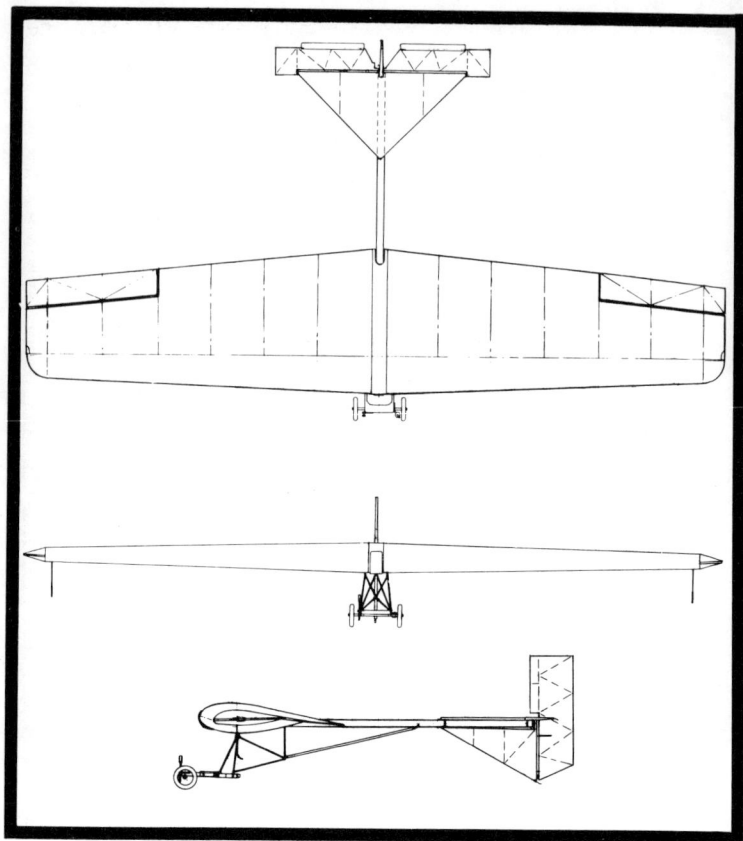

Fig. 3-12. General layout of the VJ-23 hang glider. (Courtesy Volmer Aircraft)

surface. Were canvas to be used on curved portions, it would dish-in between adjacent ribs and the true airfoil shape would be compromised. Control surfaces may also be built up in a similar fashion; however, if these surfaces are flat, they won't require built-up ribs.

Built-up structures are covered with fabric. Several applications of dope make the fabric drum-tight and impervious to weather. At areas of high stress, such as the center of the wing where the glider is joined to the fuselage, steel plates are fastened with wood screws to the spar. Bolt holes in the plates provide the necessary attachment points.

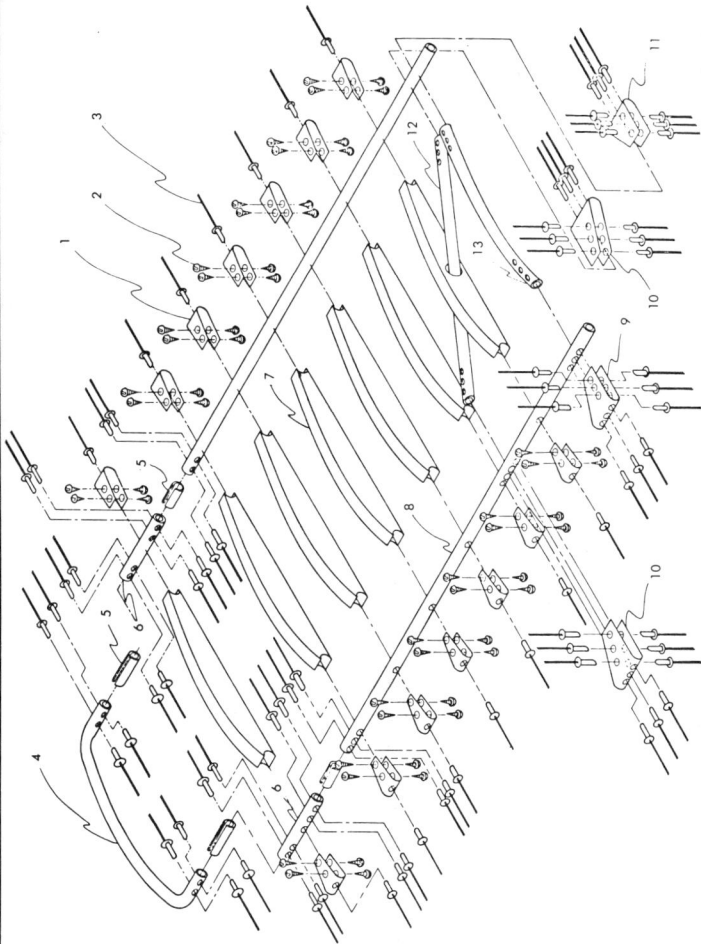

Fig. 3-13. The arrangement of wing parts in an early Icarus model. (Courtesy Ultralight Flying Machines)

67

In general, one principle prevails in aircraft structures: Stresses should be distributed as evenly as possible along and between structural members. The loads on wings are distributed over a large area (fabric), and the fabric has a long line of attachment to spars or ribs. The spars are attached to the fuselage along several points, and additional cables are used to further distribute the loads. In this manner, the entire glider serves as a "force chain"; all members bear the weight as evenly as possible.

The pilot may hang onto the glider or attach himself to it in many ways. In the old days, the pilot would simply drape his arms over two parallel bars under the wing. Later a seat, stolen from a backyard swing, was attached near the center of pressure of the wing. This way, the pilot sat comfortably, and even flew hands-off if the balance was carefully established. Most gliders have several points (usually a plate with holes in it) to which a seat can be attached with a D-link or quick-disconnect device.

It is important that the swing seat remain firmly attached to the pilot so that after a stormy takeoff he can settle down comfortably and concentrate on flying. An automobile safety belt or a rope sling can be attached to the seat; webbing can be used to hold the seat to the thighs.

Some manufacturers fabricate seats which resemble parachute harnesses. Padding is applied to pressure areas so the flier's circulation won't be cut off during long flights (Fig. 3-14).

Flying in a prone position is the ultimate thrill. Less wind resistance is met than in the seated position, resulting in a better glide. The air drag on a seated pilot is about 12 lb, while that on a prone pilot is 3 lb.

The common prone harness is much like a parachute harness and has two or more webs connected to a common attachment point on the glider. The pilot is able to make a running start and, once in the air, he can rotate into the prone position. Conventional two-point suspension makes the pilot support the weight of his legs. During long flights, this is tiresome. For this reason, many pilots fabricate their own weight suspenders, ranging from simple ribbons attached to

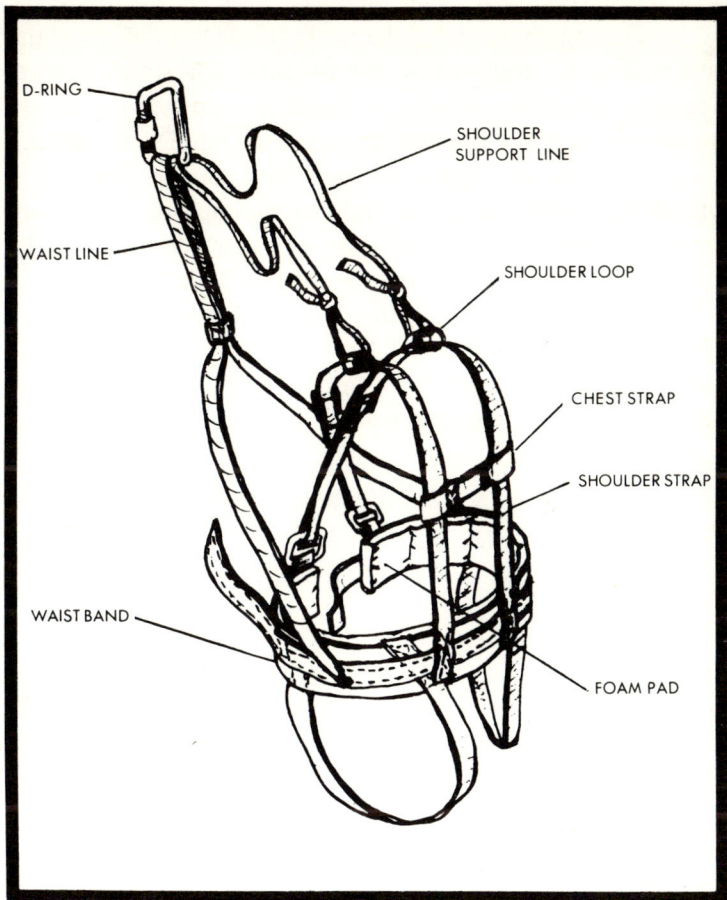

Fig. 3-14. A prone harness. (Courtesy Free Flight Systems)

each ankle, to complicated systems of bungee cords or spring-loaded webs attached to the knees, thighs, calves, and ankles. Indeed, the word web is appropriate here; a pilot so equipped ressembles a man caught in a gigantic spider web.

The harness may be attached to the pilot with buckles, double rings, or Velcro. The latter is a patented device consisting of two tapes: one with tiny loops on it and another with hooks to match. The two tapes, although the hooks and loops are firmly interlocked, can be easily ripped apart. Velcro costs about $1 per foot; expensive, but worth the price of the convenience.

I stress again that all glider parts should be made from the best materials, designed for the purpose. Use stainless steel wherever possible. Beware of surplus materials or cheap imitations. Test any new design on a small hill. Do not assume a kite is strong enough for all flight attitudes just because it withstood one straight glide; tight turns, imposing more than normal flight loads, have proved new designs to be inadequate—when aluminum tubes bent or folded.

If you have any questions, contact the Hang Glider Manufacturers' Association. Their Category 1 specifications should be followed when designing kites, and when you purchase one commercially made.

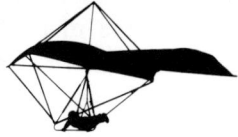

Chapter 4

Flexible Wings

You may recall the paper darts you made as a child. They sure flew well, didn't they? A triangular aircraft—pointed nose, tapered wings, and straight keel—presents inherent stability, and has flight characteristics which are very forgiving. Paper darts, thrown in the air at high speeds, soon stabilize to a slow, fluttering flight and land with aplomb. No, they don't fly as well as more elaborate, conventional configurations, but they certainly provide fun.

I presume the inspiration for Francis Rogallo was the dart when he was thinking of inventing a simple airplane. He was looking for an inherently simple, stable plane; even if it meant sacrificing the performance associated with regular gliders. He experimented with kites (paper or canvas wings stretched over a simple framework) and ultralight structures of various kinds.

In 1951 he was awarded a patent for a kite consisting of a rigid keel and a square of flexible material fastened to it along one of the diagonals. The two outboard tips of the square were tethered in such a manner that when the wind filled the "sail" the two wing panels formed cylindrical surfaces. Several wings could be fastened on top of each other to provide more lift. Francis and his wife Gertrude eventually added a spar (made from a rigid material) to each wing to provide a better, more stable framework. Experimenting with the square shape, they eventually deleted the aft tip of the rectangle; it became two triangles, joined at their hypotenuses. The result, the well known Rogallo wing, was the basis for the hang gliding movement.

71

When NASA took on the task of learning everything about the Rogallo wing, they did it with a characteristic thoroughness. They studied wing loadings, optimum configurations, wing shapes, leading-edge angles, angles of attack, positions of center of gravity, streamlines, tip vortexes—and more. They called the Rogallo wing by such names as "flex wing," "parawing," and "sailwing." They found many of their answers mathematically others, empirically (by trial and error). Even today many aspects of the Rogallo remain mysteries despite its apparent simplicity. Aerodynamically, the various elements have almost infinite

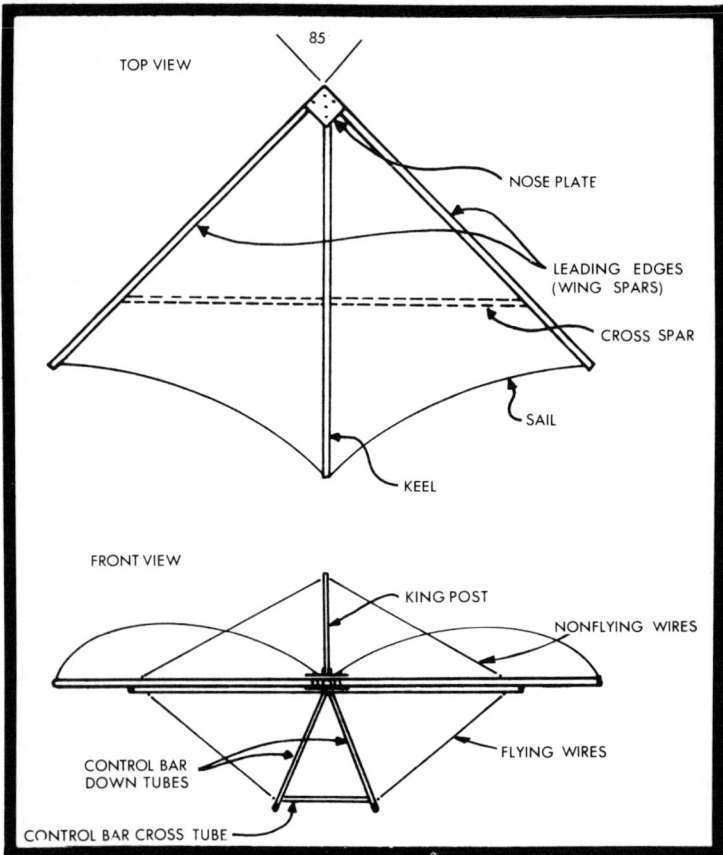

Fig. 4-1. The main elements of a standard Rogallo wing. (Courtesy Whitney Enterprises)

variations. The fact that the wing covering (plastic, in most cases) hangs loosely when the kite is not flying prompted people to call this type of airplane a "flexible wing" craft. And the fact that early models were tested as tethered kites seems to have stuck with gliders; they are still called *kites*.

To make a basic Rogallo wing, begin by taking three slender rods of equal length and tying them together at one end. Separate the outside pieces so they make a 90-degree angle; the center rod will be at a 45-degree angle to the outside rods. Cover the entire structure with a light, air-impermeable material (fastened to the rods). Next, move the outside rods closer together—decreasing the angle to about 85 degrees to provide slack for the wing material; maintain the center piece exactly between the outside pieces (Fig. 4-1). By fastening a rod (cross spar) between the approximate midpoint of the other rods (wing spars), the angles can be maintained.

The covering material will flap loosely until you lift up the structure and allow air to fill it from underneath, either by facing the wind or running into it. The free edges of the covering material will form an arc, while the rest of the sail assumes a conical shape. The two cones formed by both panels overlap (Fig. 4-2). If one of the panels were cut by a vertical plane parallel to the keel (Fig. 4-3), the resulting cross-sectional shape would resemble an airfoil. It would also be similar to the shape of birds' wings, the configuration

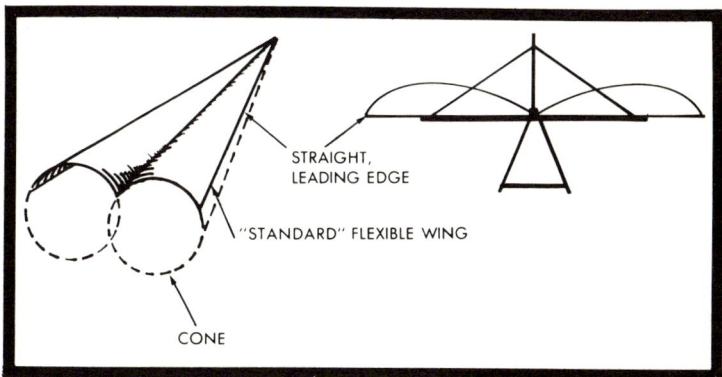

STRAIGHT, LEADING EDGE

"STANDARD" FLEXIBLE WING

CONE

Fig. 4-2. The wings of a straight, leading-edge kite generate two conical surfaces.

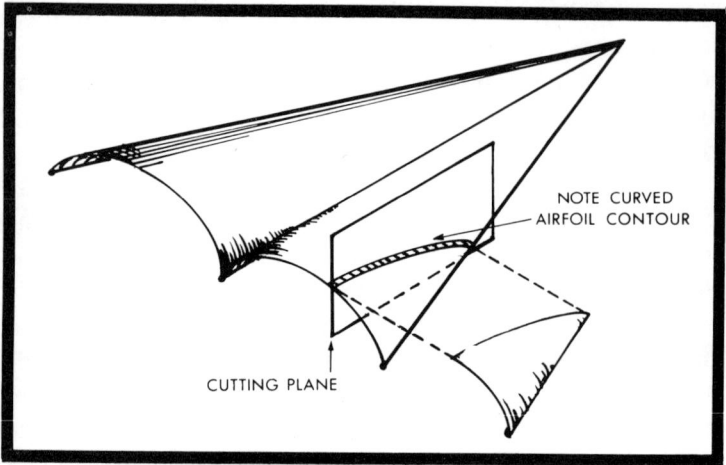

Fig. 4-3. The straight, leading-edge configuration results in a wing cross section with an airfoil shape.

developed (by trial and error) by Lillienthal, the Wright brothers, and all the aeronautical researchers since the discovery of flight.

In conventional airplanes it is seldom necessary to locate the center of gravity in the vertical plane. Stability in a Rogallo wing depends on locating the center of gravity in a vertical line. When the center of gravity is properly located—along the keel and perpendicularly below it—and the proper weight is suspended at that point, very stable flight will result. But, stability will only be maintained in a very narrow region; if the center of gravity is placed outside this region, the wing becomes unstable (Fig. 4-4). The perpendicular line going from the center of gravity on the keel connects to a vertical line extending from the nose to the ground (Fig. 4-5), resulting in an intersection point close to the ideal center of gravity. The intersection should be between $^1/_5$ and $^3/_5$ the length of the keel and below it. The vertical center of gravity location applies to a pilot suspended from the keel, hanging on to the control bar; he must be considered part of the structure. (His own center of gravity is near his waistline.)When the pilot lets go of the control bar and simply hangs from a ring (as in stunt flying), his point of suspension is really a universal joint

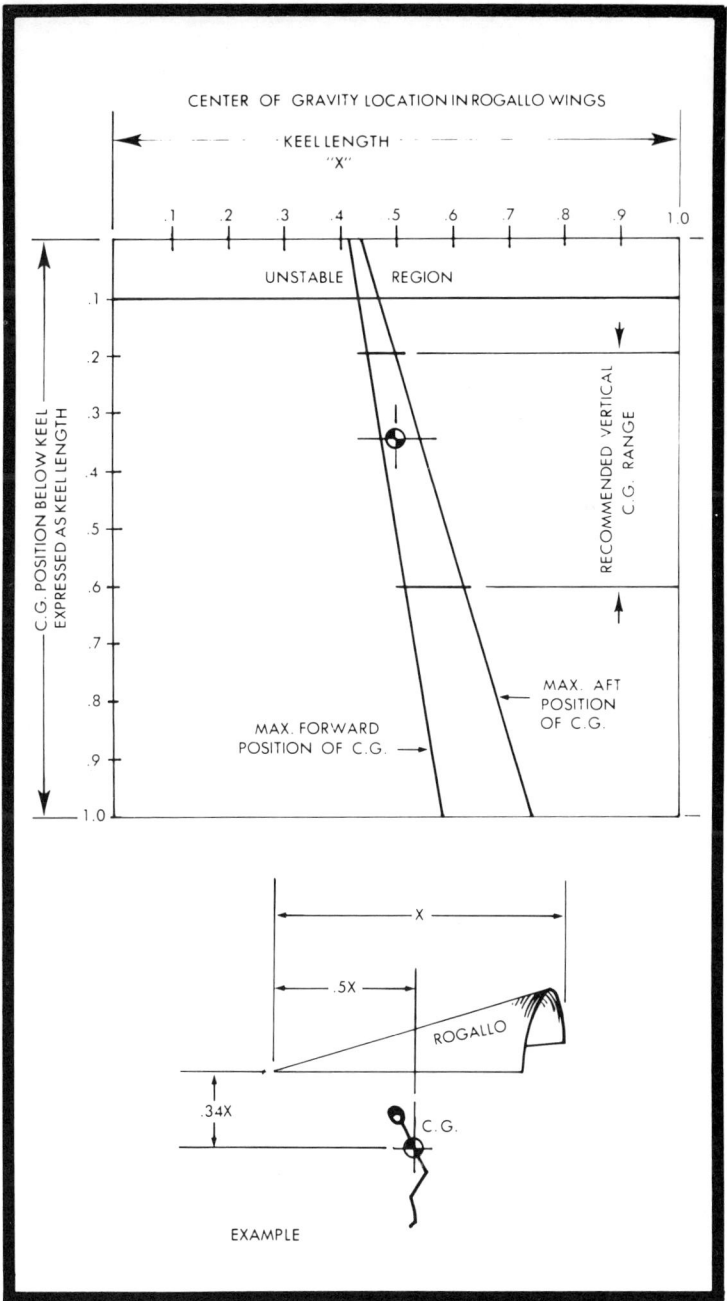

Fig. 4-4. Locating the center of gravity in Rogallo wings.

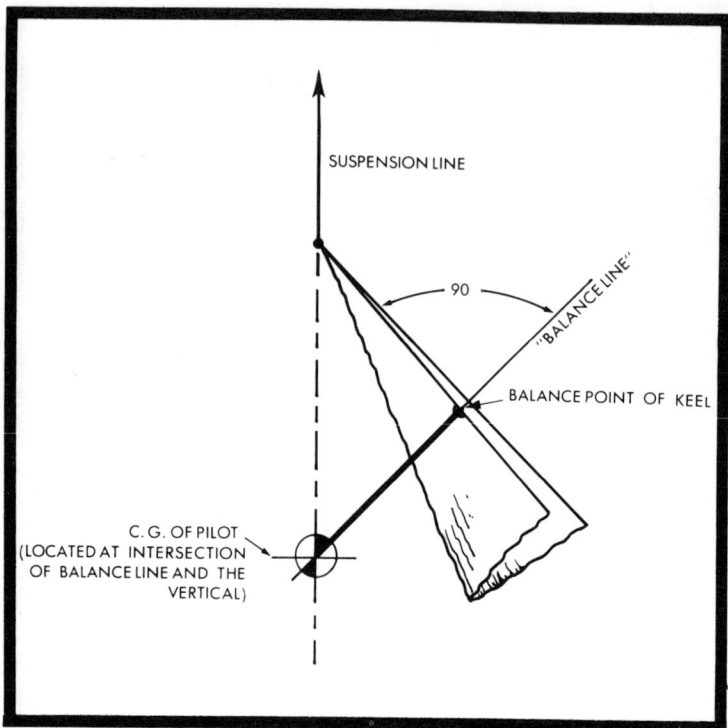

SUSPENSION LINE

90

"BALANCE LINE"

BALANCE POINT OF KEEL

C. G. OF PILOT
(LOCATED AT INTERSECTION
OF BALANCE LINE AND THE
VERTICAL)

Fig. 4-5. Finding the vertical balance point of a Rogallo wing.

and his weight can be considered to be concentrated at a point which almost coincides with the keel. This extremely high center of gravity position produces almost neutral stability with the result that the kite may be easily upset by a slight gust of air. Therefore, hold the control bar at all times. The center of gravity of the kite alone should be slightly behind the control bar, so that during takeoff the weight of the structure will produce a natural, nose-up attitude.

Weight is also important. Most orthodox airplanes only require balancing. The Rogallo wing, on the other hand, needs a certain minimum weight as a ballast for proper balance. Luckily, the minimum required is much less than the weight of a pilot; there is no need to add weight to full-size kites. The weight located below the keel acts much like a pendulum. The sails provide lift, while the weight (properly located) provides continuous control of the angle of attack as well as side-to-side stability. In proper trim, the keel is angled with its nose slightly above the horizontal: the *nominal* angle of attack. If the pilot is located very close to the keel, a very small weight shift will produce an immediate change in flight attitude. Farther from the keel, his weight shifts have a lesser effect. Center of gravity positions below the keel by up to 50% of its length, will work; but such low positions necessitate extreme control movements. A proper angle of attack insures sufficient lift with minimum drag, resulting in stable flight. Should any outside influence affect this condition, the ballast weight will move from its lowest position and create a couple which will tend to move the structure back to normal. Thus, when the flier reaches equilibrium in flight, all he has to do is hang on; minor wind gusts will be automatically compensated for. Nevertheless, to achieve a degree of control over the Rogallo wing, the relative angle between the keel and the vertical line through the weight has to be changed to set up a different angle of attack. Similarly, if the lateral angle (between the line connecting the wingtips and the vertical line through the weight) is changed, one wing will be higher than the other, the kite will develop more lift from that wing, and the kite will turn.

Another important point is that when the angle between the leading edges is increased, lift will increase rapidly while stability will decrease. If the leading-edge angle is decreased to a more arrowlike shape, less lift will be available and, therefore, flight speed will be much higher—although stability will improve tremendously. New designs have to be evaluated with these points in mind. The amount of *billow*, i.e., the upward curvature of the sails when filled with air, also determines the amount of lift and control. Today's modern, mass-produced Rogallo wings are a compromise, made mainly to accommodate pilots new to the sport who require safety more than performance.

Near the keel the wing is almost flat (in cross section), graduating to the shape of an airfoil towards the wing spars. (This can be seen in Fig. 4-1.) The cross section at the wingtips may be actually at a negative angle of attack relative to the flight path. However, the negative angle becomes positive

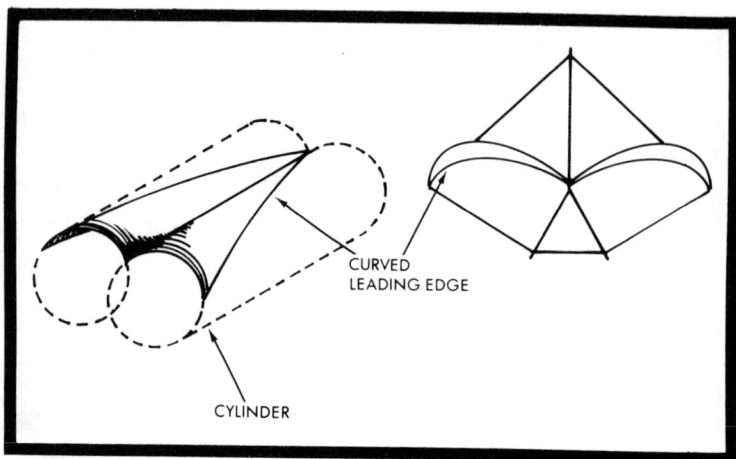

Fig. 4-6. Two cylindrical surfaces form the curved, leading edge of a flexible wing.

when the keel is pointed acutely upwards; thus, while the center of the wing is at (or beyond) the stall angle, the wingtips are still "flying." This is important; it prevents wingtip stalls when the kite is flying slowly and goes into a tight turn. The wingtip on the inside of the turn may have very little airspeed, but it still produces lift because of the low angle of attack. Without this feature, low-speed tight turns would develop into uncontrollable spins.

A late development in Rogallo wings for hang gliding is a curved leading edge which tends to make the wing panels cylindrical instead of conical. Looking at such a panel from directly in front of the glider, one only sees the thin edge of the covering (Fig. 4-6). Thus, we have arrived at the original Rogallo kite. Cylindrical wings are harder to produce because the aluminum tubes have to be bent into a precise shape (identical on both sides); but they produce more lift than conventional conical wings.

Since the wing surfaces depend on air to hold them taut in the desired shape, it is obvious that if the kite develops a negative angle of attack (as in a steep dive), there will be equal pressure above and below. The sail will become loose; in sailboat parlance, *luff*. This could easily develop into an irreversible condition, with potentially fatal consequences. To prevent this, most gliders employ one or more aids. The sail's trailing edge may be made to flex slightly upwards by tightening the rear ground wires, giving an upward, flexed shape. Another remedy is to install an auxiliary wing over the tip. This wing, with an angle of incidence higher than that of the main wing, helps pull the kite out of a dive. A third remedy is to install a small fabric surface between the rear flying wires, just under the rear tip of the keel. The angle of the wires relative to the keel provides a downwards moment at the keel, thus helping to lift the nose up in a dive.

While early hang gliders based on the Rogallo wing had wingspans of about 16 feet, they were only suitable for low, ground-skimming flights. This is because their wing loading was quite high. After much experimentation, it has been found that wing loadings of around 0.95 to 1.05 lb/sq. ft produce the best flight characteristics. Thus, for each pilot (assuming the flying attire is normal and the kite weighs about 35 pounds) there is an optimum kite size. Windspeed is also a factor. For each combination of pilot-and-windspeed, there is a best compromise. Low wing loadings mean awkward ground handling and more susceptibility to wind gusts—but better soaring performance.

The typical flexible-wing hang glider, as it is being manufactured literally by the thousands every month, has a keel tube between 16 and 20 feet long and the wingtips are 19 to 26 feet apart. The leading edges are angled at 80 to 88 degrees. The fabric is allowed to billow 2 to 4 degrees from the rest position. The structure is usually made from aluminum tubes stayed with steel cables, resulting in a structure weighing 30 to 45 pounds (Fig. 4-7).

The modern Rogallo glider usually has some kind of seat to make long flights comfortable. In some cases, the pilot reverts to a prone position (Fig. 4-8) during flight; this reduces drag by more than half. The glide ratio is usually around 4:1, with some good kites flying at close to 5:1. Latest developments in Rogallo wings promise even better glide ratios.

The sink speeds of modern Rogallo hang gliders with 1 lb/sq ft wing loading is around 7.5 ft/sec. The airspeed is

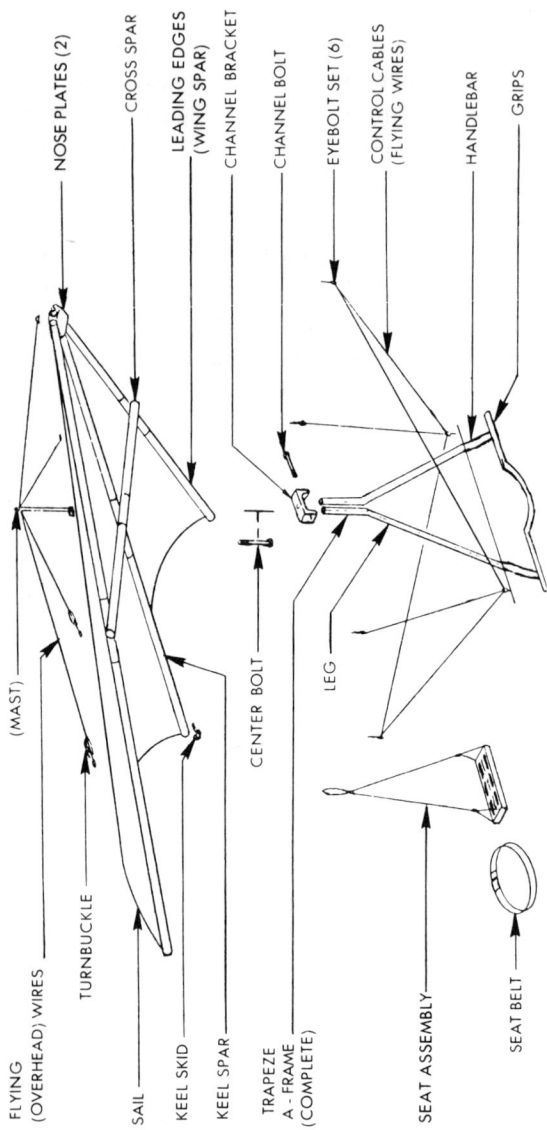

Fig. 4-7. The nomenclature for the parts of a standard, flexible-wing kite. (Courtesy Delta Wing Kites and Gliders, Inc.)

FLYING
(OVERHEAD) WIRES

TURNBUCKLE

(MAST)

NOSE PLATES (2)

CROSS SPAR

LEADING EDGES
(WING SPAR)

CHANNEL BRACKET

CHANNEL BOLT

EYEBOLT SET (6)

CONTROL CABLES
(FLYING WIRES)

HANDLEBAR

GRIPS

SAIL

KEEL SKID

KEEL SPAR

TRAPEZE
A - FRAME
(COMPLETE)

CENTER BOLT

LEG

SEAT ASSEMBLY

SEAT BELT

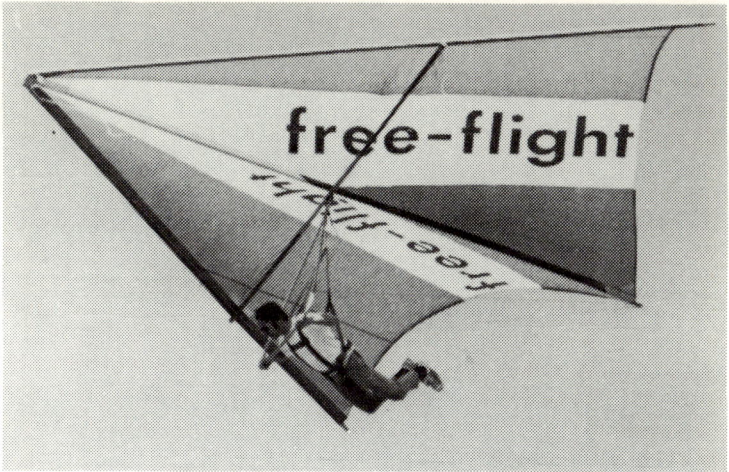

Fig. 4-8. Most advanced fliers use the prone position. This reduces air drag and improves performance.

around 20 mph. Speeds much higher than that are not tolerated well by the wing (which starts to flutter and lose lift), although speeds of around 40 mph have been attained by experienced pilots. Just about any kind of flight maneuver can be performed by Rogallos—except inverted flight. It is important to appreciate that the sail must be filled at all times to assume an airfoil shape and serve as a wing. If the kite were "stood on its nose," the sails might collapse suddenly and, lacking control surfaces, the pilot would be unable to pull out of the dive. The standard Rogallo wing has no stabilizing surfaces; it depends entirely on its delta shape to prevent the center of pressure from moving too much.

When the angle of attack of a Rogallo wing is increased considerably, the drag of the sail increases; thus, flying speed diminishes. The L/D curve for these wings has a very soft peak: as drag increases, lift is lost very gradually. This is one of the most important characteristics of the flexible wing. Its stall speed is almost zero. Thus, by lifting the nose, flying speed can be checked; and because lift is reduced, the plane can be made to sink gradually to the ground. With the proper coordination, a pilot can bring his kite to a dead-stop, standup landing. In fact, it's possible to lose altitude by simply

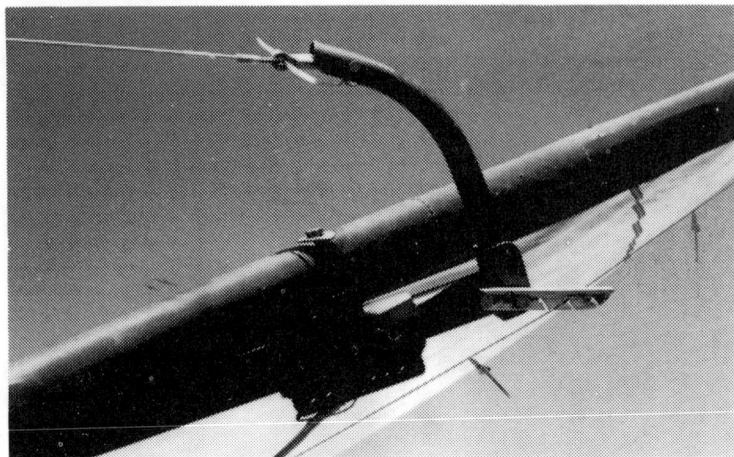

Fig. 4-9. A cable is used on this kite to reduce flexing in the leading edge. Cable tightness is controlled by the curved arm and the tightness of the nonflying wire above.

parachuting the kite; but this should only be attempted by experienced pilots, because during a severe stall, the kite could slip backwards and the sails collapse.

When the kite is near the ground, air movement under the wing may actually hit the ground. One can feel a whoosh of air when a kite flies very low, directly overhead. This downward air movement creates additional lift just prior to landing, cushioning the landing considerably.

There have been many attempts to provide additional control surfaces for kites; these included long tails, *canard* surfaces at the front to produce longitudinal control, changeable wing panels, and folding, controllable wingtips to reduce lift on one side. To date, the most successful system is the simple, weight-shift method. Properly used, weight shifting is very effective and quite foolproof.

Every part of the conventional flexible wing is stayed with cables to reinforce it against flying and landing loads. However, the extreme tips of the leading edges usually are not stayed. As a result, the upward pressure generated by the lift of the sails tends to pull the leading edge tips towards the keel; the sails lose their finely engineered billow, causing flutter, loss of lift, and loss of control. Stronger tubes can be used, but

Fig. 4-10. The entire kite folds into an easy-to-carry package.

they may be unnecessarily heavy. A better method is to connect a somewhat loose cable between the ends of the wing spar, and pull the center of the cable tightly over an arm near the point where the wing spar joins the mast (Fig. 4-9). The tightness can be controlled by cable length as well as control-arm size. This system may make the leading edge droop slightly on the ground, but when flight loads are applied to the sail, the leading edge becomes straight.

One person can assemble such a kite from a kit, or buy it assembled for $500 to $600. The kite can be folded to a 15- to 20-foot package only 6 inches in diameter (Fig. 4-10). It can be easily unloaded from a car and set up in less than 10 minutes, often without tools (Fig. 4-11). Unless the wind is very strong,

Fig. 4-11. Assembly takes but a few minutes.

Fig. 4-12. Flexible-wing kites are easy to carry and transport.

one person can carry the assembled kite to a launch site on top of a hill, and take off unassisted; without an engine or towing contrivance. When the kite's not in use, the control bar/trapeze can be left in place; but the leading edges should be rolled up smoothly to avoid damage (Fig. 4-12).

With the nose of the kite stuck in the ground to prevent it from being blown away, the sail serves as a sun shield or tent. Many people—fliers, their families, and friends—picnic under the kite between flights (Fig. 4-13).

Fig. 4-13. With its nose stuck in the sand, a flexible-wing kite makes an ideal shelter for picnicking.

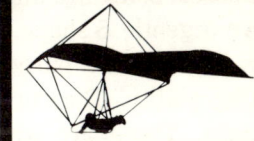

Chapter 5

Fixed Wings

Since time immemorial men have examined the wings of fallen birds to find out what made them fly. They discovered that the cross section of the wings was curved. When they tried to duplicate bird's wings, and tested their models in wind tunnels, they found that the curved surface was the reason for the wings' superior lifting ability. When experimental wings were built to have some thickness as well, it was found that some thickness in the forward part of the airfoil further contributed to lift.

In trying to achieve flight, most early pioneers constructed aircraft with wings of a definite structure, over which canvas was stretched to form the desired curved surface. Such planes have wings that do not need to be filled by wind to form a flying surface; for this reason, hang gliders which have wings with a definite curvature in the direction of flight are called *fixed wing* gliders.

A conventional wing generates lift because of the "suction" created by air speeding over it; the lift comes from the greater air pressure under the wing. Obviously, the faster the air moves over the wing, the more lift is generated. At the same time, however, the faster the wing moves, the more drag it generates. The amount of drag depends on the angle of attack and the shape of the airfoil. Depending on the drag produced by the various parts of the airplane and the pilot's body, the total drag has to be overcome by the gravity-produced (glide angle) speed of the plane. For each set of conditions there is a limit to the speed the plane can achieve. It is the designer's job to design the plane so that the lift produced is sufficient to keep the plane in the air. For a particular weight (pilot and plane) and drag condition, there is an optimum airfoil for best flying characteristics. There are a large number of airfoils available, developed for a variety of purposes. Some are almost flat; some are quite curved. Some have a gentle S shape. Some are thin; some are thick. Each has a particular purpose, such as speed, speed range, and lifting ability. The curvatures are plotted as coordinates on graphs. These are available in books devoted to aviation science, and NASA booklets. An airfoil which does a good job for a transport plane would never do for a fighter plane. Similarly, conventional airfoils will not do for hang gliders because of the lower speeds involved. Low-speed flight, as it applies to ultralight hang gliders, requires special study in the area of airfoils, angles of attack, stall speeds, etc. We are just making inroads in this area; low-speed flight has been neglected during the past five decades.

Low-speed light planes seem to perform best when the airfoil has a considerable curvature. The maximum curvature should be in the first 30% to 40% of the airfoil's cross section, from front to back. If more extensive workmanship can be mustered, and additional weight tolerated, the wing can be built up from bits and pieces of wood into a thick section to produce more lift.

Fixed-wing airplanes may have one or two sets of wings. A *monoplane* must be very strong to withstand the stresses of flight and landing. Cantilevered structures (with members supported at one end) are seldom strong enough; they must be stayed with external wires. If two sets of wings are used, wires can be strung between them in a crisscross fashion to provide the necessary strength. In this case, the wing structure has to be just strong enough to hold its basic shape; the stresses are taken up mainly by the wires and struts. Let us examine this closely.

A monoplane hang glider is shown at the top of Fig. 5-1. There are two sets of wires on each side of the wing. The wires (called X wires) support the wings in flight; they are in tension when the plane is in flight. The struts of the triangular control bar are in compression; the lower ends of the X wires pull up

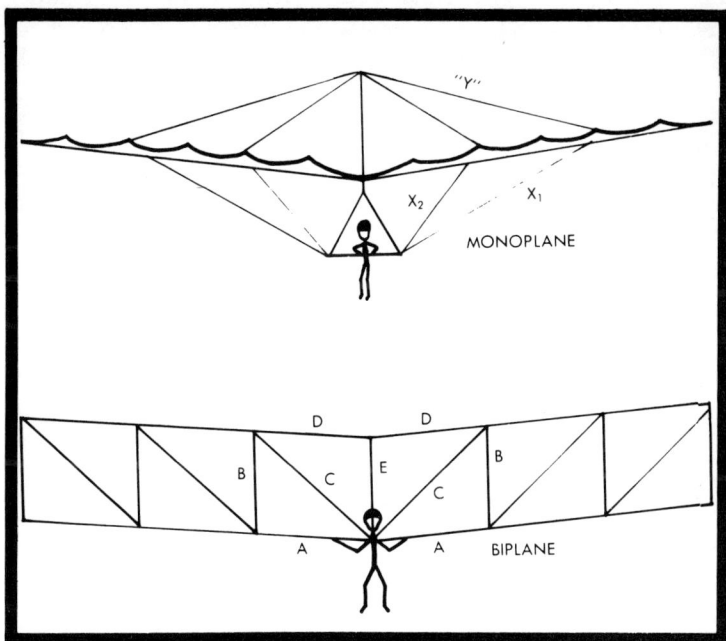

Fig. 5-1. Monoplane glider (top) and biplane glider (bottom). Note the position of the wire rigging.

on them. Two or more sets of flying wires may be used (designated X_1 and X_2) if the wing is very long. Each wire supports one wing section. There are always two sets of wires at each rib: one fastened to the leading edge; the other, to the trailing edge. This is done to prevent the wing from twisting when aerodynamic loads exert pressure on it from below.

During landing and storage the wings would tend to droop downwards without Y wires. These wires are fastened to the top of the wing in a fashion similar to that used for the flying wires. During flight the Y wires are loose. They only become tight because of wind gusts or landing pressure. The triangulated structure of the wing relieves the main wing spars of some of the stresses also.

With a biplane, the situation is somewhat different. Typical biplane rigging is shown on the bottom of Fig. 5-1. Wing panel A has air pressure on it, pointing upwards. The amount of pressure is somewhere between 10 and 20 pounds, distributed over the surface evenly. An average wing panel measures about 3 by 5 feet, and the wing loading is approximately 1 lb/sq ft. The outboard edge of the wing panel presses upwards against the bottom of the solid strut, B. The top of strut B is connected to the upper wing panel (D) and bracing wire C. Wing panel D pulls upwards on the end of wire C and strut E. There are two triangles involved here: ABC and CDE. In each case, bracing wire C is in tension when the plane is in flight. Another wire crosses C (not shown) to serve as a *landing wire* to take up loads on the wing in the opposite direction. It is important to realize that the aluminum tubes, or wooden members, are relatively weak and the joints of the wing panels and struts are not reinforced in any particular way (e.g., with extra brackets). Yet the structure is very rigid because of cross bracing. This can be demonstrated easily by forming a quadrangle from wooden rods connected with hinges. Such a structure is loose. When opposite corners are connected with equal lengths of wire, the structure becomes very rigid. If two wing panels are mounted on top of each other, and cross braced between opposite corners, the structure acts like a rigid box and will resist warping. Thus, either individual members have to be very strong, or they have to be braced with wires (Fig. 5-2). The penalties one pays for wire bracing is additional drag and complexity. These factors are tolerable in hang gliders—easily reparable, low-cost structures.

Drag can be reduced somewhat if the vertical struts are streamlined. Struts, usually made from tubing or wood to resist buckling (they are mostly in compression), can be streamlined with the addition of a cardboard fairing. Frayed wires, or large-diameter ropes, create quite a lot of air resistance. It is best to use thin, steel wires or aircraft-quality cables. Plastic coatings further reduce drag.

Why don't all planes have two sets of wings? Don't two wings provide twice as much lift as one wing? Not quite. There is interaction between two wings. The high-pressure side of the upper wing faces the low pressure side of the lower wing. As a result, some of the potential lift is lost. The *downwash* of the upper wing affects the lower wing. For these reasons, it is best

Fig. 5-2A. Landing wires on a biplane and flying wires on a biplane.

to stagger the two wings with the lower one displaced slightly rearward. This ideal position is difficult to achieve on homemade gliders and, as a result, most biplane hang-glider wings are placed one directly above the other.

Now let us discuss the basic aerodynamics of the conventional glider. The so-called conventional glider has a

Fig. 5-2B. The flying wires.

wing (or wings) up front and a smaller rear surface connected to the wing(s) by a fuselage. The *main wing* supplies lift to hold the plane in the air. As the wing develops lift, it tends to assume a greater angle of attack. When the angle of attack increases, the center of aerodynamic pressure (where the lift is assumed to be concentrated) moves rearwards from a normal position. The normal position for the center of pressure is on the chord, usually about one-third the distance from the leading edge. With an increased angle of attack the center of pressure moves towards the trailing edge, lifting the leading edge, and if left unchecked, causing the wing to flip. In order to keep the angle of attack constant relative to the flight path, a horizontal stabilizer is mounted on the end of the fuselage. The horizontal stabilizer need be no larger than one-fifth the area of the wing; and, the farther from the wing, the smaller the area it has to have. Thus, the product of the moment arm (the distance from the center of pressure to the stabilizer) and the stabilizer area can be considered constant. Its action is simple. If the wing rises in the front, the angle of the fuselage changes and so does the angle of attack of the stabilizer with respect to the flight path. As soon as the stabilizer assumes a positive angle of attack (its leading edge higher than the trailing edge) it develops lift and, thus, lifts the tail. This in turn lowers the leading edge of the wing; equilibrium is restored. The opposite happens when the leading edge of the wing dips to a negative angle of attack. This action-and-reaction happens constantly, and automatic correction is applied instantly; the plane flies in dynamic balance. In most planes, the stabilizer's angle of attack is zero: it is aligned with the airstream. If you look at such a plane from directly in front, you will see the front edge of the stabilizer. The wing is set at a slight angle of attack, usually 5 to 10 degrees, to produce the best compromise between lift and drag.

Directional stability is insured by the rudder and the dihedral angle. The dihedral angle is the angle between the wings and the horizontal in level flight when viewed from the front (Fig. 5-3). It is fortunate that natural aerodynamic loads tend to cause the wingtips to bow upwards. This, combined with the loaded condition, produces a dihedral of about 5

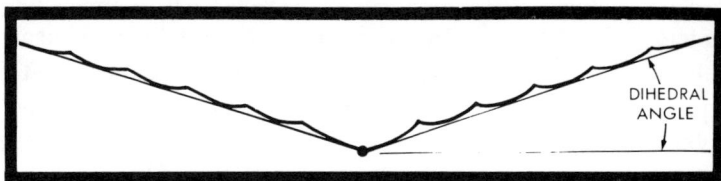

Fig. 5-3. The dihedral angle.

degrees in most planes. Should one wing be pushed forward without actually executing a turn, it will create more drag than the backward wing and hold the forward wing back. Stability is achieved automatically.

Another advantage of having a slight dihedral angle built into the wings is the compensation for one wing being lower than the other. This may be caused by a sudden wind gust. If there was no dihedral angle, the lower wing would slip down; equilibrium would have to be restored by ailerons or by the pilot shifting his weight. This would take a very alert pilot who would have to constantly concentrate on flying. The dihedral angle compensates for a low wing by simply exposing a larger wing area on the low side. Looking at Fig. 5-4, it can be seen that the lower wing has a larger plan (projected) area than the higher wing. This causes the lower wing to develop more lift, restoring equilibrium automatically.

The most important advantage of having a dihedral angle is automatic banking when the plane enters a turn. When the

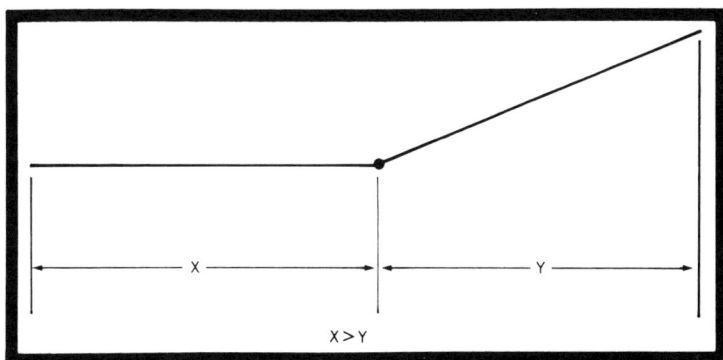

Fig. 5-4. How the dihedral angle keeps the plane on an even keel. Y is shorter than X; hence, Y will sink and X will rise.

rudder is applied, the tail develops *horizontal lift* and turns sideways. At this point, the outside wing presents more of its underside to the airstream than does the inside wing. The outside wing flies at an angle of attack higher than that of the inside wing; thus, it develops more lift. The result is that the outside wing lifts up higher and the plane banks automatically towards the center of the turn. Also, the outside wing creates more drag than the other wing, causing the outside wing to drag backwards and counteract the yaw. In regular planes the ailerons counteract this tendency, but in hang gliding simplicity is more important than a theoretically correct turning attitude.

Control of a fixed-wing hang glider is achieved mainly by the pilot shifting his weight. The tail and fuselage are so light that if the pilot shifts his weight a few inches fore or aft, the equilibrium of the plane is drastically altered. For this reason, most fixed-wing gliders don't have movable elevators. However, turning must be augmented with a movable rudder.

The rudder, a vertical surface usually located behind the stabilizer, acts much like the rudder on a boat. When the rudder is deflected, it meets more pressure on that side. This moves the tail to the other side. Combined with the banking action produced by the dihedral angle, this results in a smoothly executed turn. Most simple, fixed-wing gliders use rudders in which the entire surface moves, and which are connected by control cables, running on pulleys, to the pilot's seat. Thus, any weight shift automatically moves the rudder in the proper direction.

The rudder is slanted in a tight turn. If the rudder remained completely vertical, it would only produce a sideways motion in the tail without affecting its up-and-down movement. In a pronounced bank the tail is lifted up towards the outside of the turn and the plane tends to nose-in, or tighten the turn. In a normal airplane this could be compensated for by applying up-elevator and reducing rudder; in a hang glider, this cannot be done, as a rule. Judicious application of the rudder is, therefore, very necessary when flying a simple, fixed-wing hang glider.

The slender wings of the fixed-wing glider develop more lift and less drag than a Rogallo wing. At the wingtips the negative pressure (on top) and the positive pressure (on the bottom) "leak out" and mix, causing a swirling air movement called a *vortex*. The longer the wings, the less relative effect tip-leaks will have. This is the reason for the long, slender wings on high-performance gliders. It is especially important to cover, as much as possible, the opening in the center of the wing to prevent air leaks; it is unfortunate, in a way, to have to provide room for a pilot there.

Fixed-wing gliders are obviously more complex and heavier than flexible-wing gliders. This is why they cost more and take longer to build. It also takes at least two people to assemble them. One man has to support each end of the wing so it doesn't blow away in the wind. It is also best to have a helper hole a wingtip or the tail when launching a fixed-wing glider.

Perhaps the simplest example of these gliders is the one designed by Jack Lambie. His intent was to design a plane which could be built by just about anyone for no more than $50, and which would fly very slowly. The plane was to be light, and was not intended to fly very high. Plans for the plane appeared in *Soaring* magazine in 1970, and on the cover of *Sports Planes* in 1971. The response was tremendous. People literally begged for the plans to build their own Hang Loose. The parts are simple wooden forms made of pine, sitka spruce, or douglas fir; most are ¾ inch thick. Bamboo poles form the fuselage. Simple parts, such as bailing wire, white glue, masking tape, and cardboard are used on the remainder. The wing covering can be cheap plastic or doped canvas. To build it you need only a large garage, lots of patience, simple tools, a friend to help, and some courage.

The Hang Loose is a simple biplane having a wingspan of 28 feet. The instructions come in a simple, humorously written booklet that anyone with some common sense can understand. Triangulated wire bracing supplies strength for the wings. Alternate methods of wing rib construction are also listed, such as wrapping masking tape around plastic foam.

Fig. 5-5. Art Powell's Aeolus, a biplane hang glider.

You can order the plans from Jack Lambie, Aerodyne Co., 9460 East Artesia Blvd., Bellflower, CA 90706. Slides and pictures of the Hang Loose may still be available from Don Dwiggins, 3816 Paseo Hidalgo, Malibu, CA.

The next step up from a completely home-built biplane (Fig. 5-5) is a commercially produced monoplane. The first one of this type was designed by Bob Lovejoy, who wanted to create a simple, high-performance glider which would fold up easily for car-top transport. Other models soon followed the original Quicksilver.

Modern monoplane hang gliders are usually made from aluminum tubes, pop-riveted together. The wing ribs are also made from bent tubes, covered on top with Dacron. The fuselage consists of two tubes leading back to the tail section, stayed with steel cables for rigidity. The stabilizer is a simple, rectangular tube structure covered with Dacron. A rudder, hinged behind the stabilizer, is actuated by moving the pilot's seat. Guy wires are used to brace the wing. A conventional, triangular control bar is suspended below the wing. The pilot sits in a seat and hangs onto the bar in conventional fashion. Eipper-Formance Inc. (Box 246, Lomita, CA 90717) sells the complete plane as well as a kit for home construction.

The Conquest (Fig. 5-6) has a wingspan of 32 feet and a chord of 52 inches. It weighs approximately 60 pounds complete with wheels. It can be flown at 16 to 20 mph. The wing area is approximately 134 sq ft. The best pilot weight is around 130 lb. Heavy pilots find that can they fly faster than their lighter fellows, in this one. The glide ratio is claimed to be more than 8:1.

The most deluxe of them all s the VJ-23, truly the Cadillac of hang gliders (Fig. 5-7). Designed by experienced home-builder Vollmer Jensen, a 63-year-old Burbank man, and Irv Culver, retired Lockheed aerodynamicist, this model has the highest performance—and cost.

Vollmer Jensen has a background rich in light-aircraft design and construction. He built a two-seat, conventional glider in 1940. After WW II he designed and built the VJ-21, a personal light plane; the VJ-22 amphibian plane that followed has been in use the world over. Vollmer's first hang glider was built from *Popular Mechanics* plans in 1925. The advent of the Rogallo wing revitalized his desire to build an ultralight, simple glider (Fig. 5-8). He called upon his friend Irv Culver to

Fig. 5-6. The conquest, a fixed-wing monoplane glider. (Courtesy Conquest Hang Gliders, Inc.)

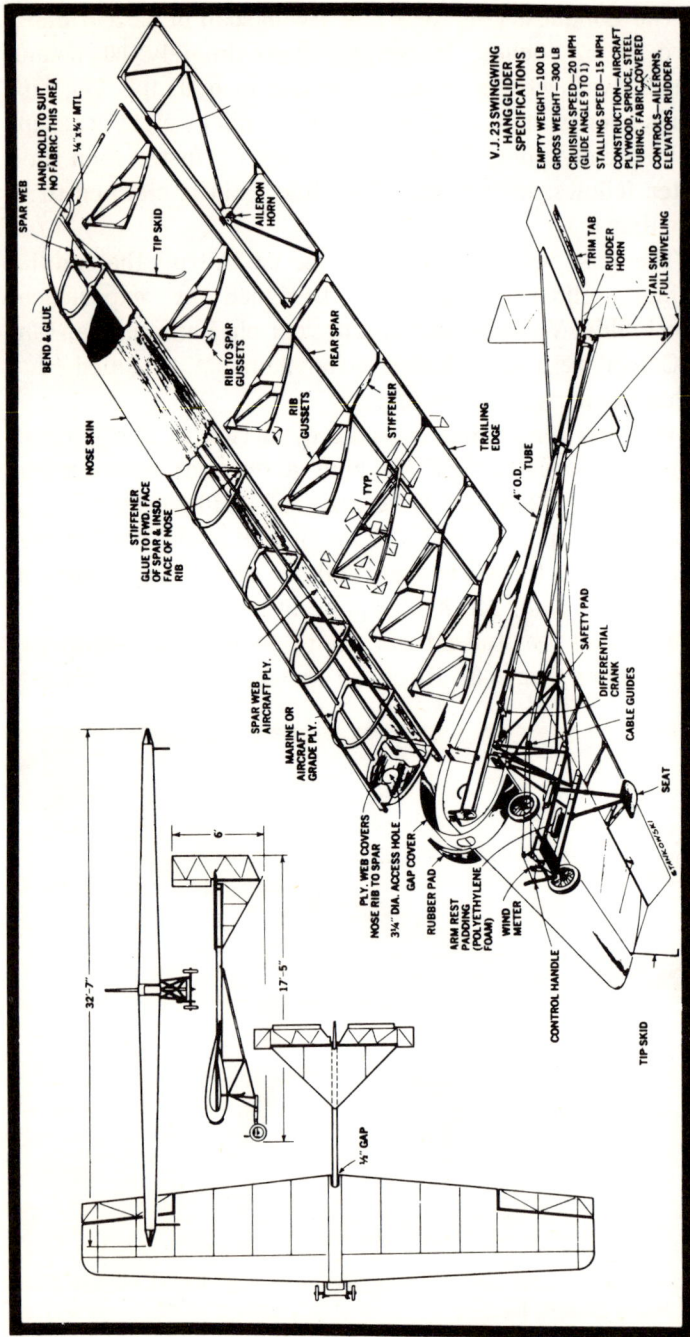

Fig. 5-7. The VJ-23 "Swingwing," designed by Volmer Jensen. (Courtesy Volmer Aircraft)

Fig. 5-8. The VJ-11, an elementary biplane glider. (Courtesy Volmer Aircraft)

Fig. 5-9. The VJ-23 can even fly off small hills. (Courtesy Volmer Aircraft)

design an airfoil for very slow flight. The result of this study: a very thick airfoil which is quite short, and terminates in a thin section much like the flaps on a large plane. They chose an aluminum boom, 4 inches in diameter, for the fuselage and a built-up, fully controllable tail section. The wing had a 32 ft span, and the entire plane weighed about 100 lb. They even designed a simple joystick to provide true, three-axis control for ailerons, elevator, and rudder. This is because they realized early in the project that simple weight-shifting was not sufficient for a large and relatively heavy glider.

Initial tests of the VJ-23 amazed not only the builders, but the onlookers as well. In the early days of hang gliding, the Rogallo wings used to merely skim a few feet over the ground. Then came Jensen. He actually soared over small sand dunes (Fig. 5-9). One of the first flights was 42 minutes long. The takeoff was easy: a few steps were taken and the craft rose like a graceful bird. *Mechanix Illustrated* published the plans in April 1973. Enthusiastic hobbyists reported fantastic success with the VJ-23. Airline pilots, plumbers, and teachers built this plane during long, winter evenings. Their efforts were rewarded with flights lasting much longer than could be had with Rogallo wings under comparable conditions.

Early in 1974, Vollmer Jensen produced the VJ-24, a slightly improved version of the earlier model (Fig. 5-10). It incorporated the latest metal-working techniques and aerodynamic features. This model took nearly 200 hours to build; but once finished, it required no tools at all to assemble. Jensen, weighing 135 pounds, takes a mere few steps to become airborne (Fig. 5-11). Landings are made at little more than jogging speed. The flight of this amazing plane is birdlike; it soars over the gentlest hills, taking advantage of the slightest thermals. The controls are light and sensitive; much like those used for real planes. The pilot drapes his arms over two parallel bars and sits on a small, circular plywood seat suspended by a single rope from the main structure.

There is little similarity between the VJ models and Rogallo wings. Were it not for the pilot's exposed position, the VJ-24 could very well be a high-performance glider, flying among the clouds like its brothers costing thousands of dollars.

Fig. 5-10. Volmer Jensen takes off in the VJ-24. (Courtesy Volmer/Aircraft)

Jensen gliders, retailing for about $1500, are manufactured by DSK Aircraft in Pacoima, California. Plans, available from Vollmer himself, include full-size templates, several sheets of blueprints, and 24 photographs. You can get information and pictures by writing to: Vollmer Aircraft, Box 5222, Glendale, CA 91201.

Fixed-wing, tailless hang gliders have an entirely different structure and aerodynamic basis than conventional tail-equipped models. They are called *all-wing* or tailless gliders. The wing cross section of such gliders is also curved to provide lift. Longitudinal stability, however, is not provided by a conventional horizontal stabilizer and rudder. Tailless gliders have *sweepback* in the wings and a *reflex airfoil.*

Sweepback refers to the blunt V shape of the wing. This provides stabilization fore and aft, as well as laterally. The airfoil is curved on the forward part; closer to the trailing edge, the curvature reverses. This is called *reflex.* The trailing edge of the wing is higher than the leading edge near the tips of the wing. This is called *washout.* The combined effect of these factors keeps the wing flying without dipping up and down.

The theory behind all this is quite interesting. The center of the wing is located forward of the wingtips. Also, the center of the wing is set at a positive angle of attack; this provides lift. As the center develops lift, the center of pressure moves towards the trailing edge, raising the leading edge further; soon it starts to get close to a stalling condition. When the forward part of the wing reaches a position where it has a tendency to flip over backwards, the wingtips begin to lift; they are now flying at a normal angle of attack. The wingtip lift produces a forward pitching moment, causing the nose to drop to a normal flying attitude. This effect takes place when the plane is in a pronounced nose-up attitude. During normal flight, the negative wingtip lift, coupled with the effect of sweepback, provides a constant forward, pitching moment; this keeps the plane in dynamic balance.

Sweepback has a yaw stabilizing effect. If the plane suddenly points to the left, the right wing will face the airstream squarely; thus, the left wing slants backwards, has less area exposed to the onrushing air, and produces less drag.

Fig. 5-11. The VJ-24 in flight. (Courtesy Volmer Aircraft)

Increased drag on the right wing pulls it back; the plane's directional stability is restored.

One of the main advantages of tailless gliders is their extreme shortness. This comes in handy when trying to take off from the face of a steep hill. Running down a hill, a tailless glider can be rotated into the proper flying position; a conventional (fuselage-and-tail) fixed-wing glider would drag its tail on the ground, probably requiring an assistant.

Directional control of tailless gliders is usually achieved by rudders located at the wingtips. When one is deflected it creates drag on that side, causing the plane to turn. When both are deflected, simultaneously, they cause enough drag to slow the plane. They act as air brakes.

One of the simplest of all hang gliders is the Sailwing designed by Mike Flannigan. Mike intended an absolutely simple hang glider which could be used to glide down from hilltops. The plans are available from Mike Flannigan, 20560 Summerville, Excelsior, MN 55331.

The Sailwing has a span of 32 ft, a wing area of 136 sq ft, and weighs 44 lb. Its glide ratio is said to be about 10:1. It can be built in about 25 hours for less than $100. Mike considers it the most flying fun for the money. He should know; he's a member of the Experimental Aircraft Association, as well as the Soaring Society of America. The Sailwing has an extremely simple aluminum-tube structure with 30 degrees of sweepback and 6 degrees of tip washout. It can be built upside-down on a garage floor.

Taras Kiceniuk Jr., an engineering student whose father has always been very interested in flight, designed a tailless glider about 4 years ago. With it, he set several world records at Torrey Pines, California. The first effort was, more or less, a prototype. The second model, Icarus II (Fig. 5-12), is a tailless biplane with approximately 30 degrees of sweepback. The wing ribs have a gentle curvature to provide lift. The ribs are covered on top with Dacron. Small deflector tips between the wings (at the extreme wingtips) are used either as rudders or airbrakes. Most wingtip rudders are hinged at about one-third the distance back from their leading edge. If they were hinged *at* the leading edge they would require

Fig. 5-12. The Icarus II. (Courtesy Ultralight Flying Machines)

considerable effort to deflect. With one-third of the rudder
surface located in front of the hinge line, the air pressure on
the forward part of the rudder supplies some of the turning
effort required. Each deflector is actuated independently by
the pilot who hangs from two padded bars in the center of the
lower wing. The Icarus II is available in kit form from:
Ultralight Flying Machines, Box 59, Cupertino, CA 95014.

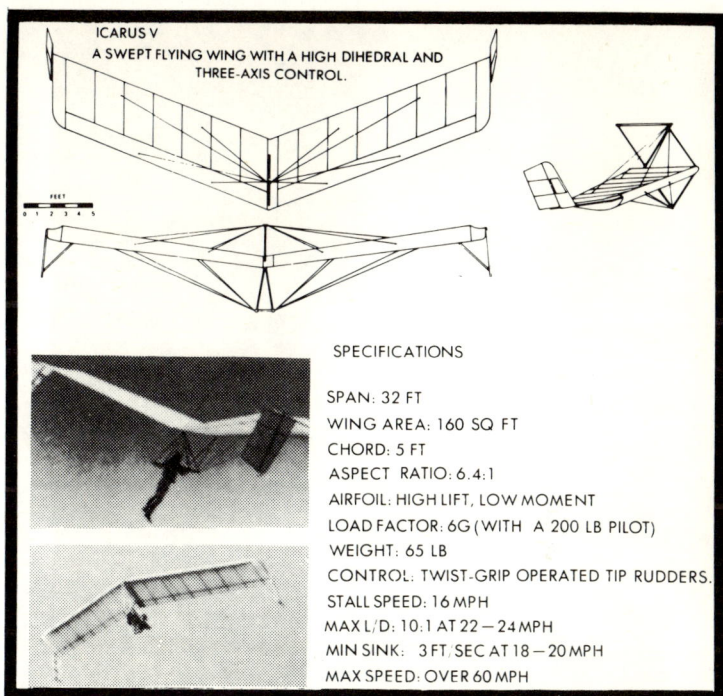

Fig. 5-13. Technical details of the Icarus V. (Courtesy Ultralight Flying Machines)

Larry Mauro, the president of the company, is a hang-glider pilot himself.

After considerable experimentation, Taras improved the performance of his tailless gliders. The latest model, Icarus V, bears little resemblance to earlier models. The Icarus V has a wingspan of 32 ft with a wing area of 160 sq ft. The aspect ratio is 6.4:1. The wing, with a built-up cross section, is quite a thick airfoil. It carries its own spar inside; this, plus the external bracing wires, produce a load factor of 6g. The plane is quite heavy as hang gliders go—65 lb—but the lift generated by the thick wing is tremendous. (Pilots as heavy as 200 pounds have flown this model.) The calculated stall speed is 16 mph; the maximum speed, nearly 60 mph. The L/D ratio is 10:1 and the sink speed is 3 ft/sec (see Fig. 5-13).

The Icarus V has rudders actuated independently by the pilot (Fig. 5-14) who uses twist grips (like motorcycle

Fig. 5-14. The Icarus V in flight. (Courtesy Ultralight Flying Machines)

throttles). When both rudders are used simultaneously, they serve as airbrakes to slow the landing speed.

Taras Jr. likes to have an assistant hold the wingtip during takeoff. Airborne, he puts his feet on the forward cross spar, which gives him a very low frontal profile. He extends his legs for landings. Preliminary plans for the Icarus V are available from Taras Kiceniuk Jr., Palomar Mountain, CA 92060.

A fixed-wing glider is not quite as easy to transport as a flexible-wing glider. The rudder stabilizer are left in one piece. But they are taken apart and removed from the twin booms of the fuselage. The wing can be taken apart in the center, sometimes in four sections. The wing sections are joined by aluminum sleeves, and the rest of the plane is held together with conventional wire cables. Many glider pilots build a huge box and mount it on top of their truck or car to carry the wings in complete safety (Fig. 5-15).

Fixed-wing gliders have a certain minimum stall speed. This means that when the airspeed of a fixed-wing glider is reduced to where the lift is less than the weight, the plane will cease to fly—it will fly uncontrollably. Below the stall speed the controls are ineffective and sufficient flying speed must be regained (actually, by falling) to regain control. Flexible-wing gliders are more forgiving in this respect.

Once the flier sees or experiences a stall he will do everything possible to avoid one. Fixed-wing gliders are

Fig. 5-15. Fixed wing gliders are usually transported in trailers.

Fig. 5-16. The Super Floater; a new breed of foot-launched glider. To land, the pilot extends his feet or touches down on a skid or wheel. (Courtesy Mountain Green Sailwing Company)

especially vulnerable; during a stall one of the wings may drop off, resulting in an edgewise dropoff, or spiral dive.

Since the average stall speed of fixed-wing gliders is above 15 mph, the landing speed is fairly high—a fast run. Because of this, only experienced pilots should fly fixed-wing gliders. It takes experience to detect and avoid an impending stall; it also takes experience to land a glider at 15 mph without suffering a broken ankle. (The combination of the speed and the mass of the glider add up to a kinetic energy which is difficult to dissipate.)

An interesting new development in foot-launched, fixed-wing gliders is the Super Floater, a product of the Mountain Green Sailwing Company (Box 771, Morgan, UT

Fig. 5-17. The Twinboomer from the Mountain Green Sailwing Company.

84050). Klaus Hill and Larry Hall designed the 90 lb high-performance glider. The pilot holds it between his legs for launching, but once in the air he puts his feet on a curved bar in front of him. Thus, the pilot sits in a semireclined position and the glider resembles the elementary trainers of 40 years ago. Plans are being made for a fully enclosed pilot.

The Super Floater has a wingspan of 32 ft, an aspect ratio of 7.35:1, and is 16 ft in length. The rudder and elevator are controlled by a joystick. In the enclosed-cockpit version, the pilot would be able to use his feet through holes at both sides of the fuselage. Although the plane is relatively heavy, and the pilot has to straddle the fuselage, he can easily foot-launch because the plane lifts in the slightest breeze; this is truly the forerunner of a new breed of gliders. The same company also produces the Twinboomer (Fig. 5-17), a glider that uses two tubes for a fuselage.

As the experience of hang glider pilots increases, many of them will want to graduate from Rogallo wings to higher performance fixed-wing gliders. Today, the latter comprise about 5% of the hang gliders in the air, but in the near future they will assume an increasingly important role.

Chapter 6

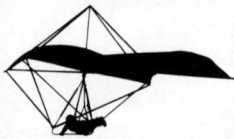

Elementary Flying Techniques

You board the multimillion-dollar airliner and settle comfortably in a plush seat. The smiling stewardess offers you a martini before takeoff. The doors close, you buckle up, and as you lean back to read the paper you hear the whine of the engines as they lift the plane into the air; you're flying. Flying? You might as well be on a bus to Topeka, Kansas—so subtle is the sensation. If they drew the curtains and woke you from a deep sleep, you'd never guess you were among the clouds.

Jack Lambie, one of America's hang gliding pioneers, once said that hang gliding is the only sport that gives a real feeling of flying. You seem to be part of the air, sensing every puff of wind. You become one with a brandnew element. You fly like a bird when you take off.

The pioneers of the sport put together contraptions they were not really sure would support a man in the air. Nobody could tell them how to fly their craft; pilots had no experience with hang gliders. Most landings were controlled crashes.

Then, a few guys succeeded in skimming a few inches over the ground. But it seemed like thousands of feet. Gradually, they were able to stay aloft for over a minute; then five minutes. They soon became the "experts." They didn't have much experience, nor did they know what they were doing; right or wrong. They merely got up, dusted themselves off, and tried again. Flights became longer and the pioneers found themselves surrounded by excited enthusiasts who wanted to experience the thrill themselves. Instruction in those days consisted of a few breathless words of advice, and maybe a diagram scratched in the dust.

Today the situation is different: theory is becoming more solid. If you have the money, you can easily buy a kite. Instructors will teach you, in a day or two, how to fly and land safely.Flying schools are springing up everywhere.There is no excuse for not taking advantage of good, safe instruction. Even if you live miles from the nearest flying school, some hang glider manufacturers will send a qualified instructor to your area (if you can guarantee a certain minimum number of students).

This chapter can't teach you to fly. I would be irresponsible if I claimed it could. If you believe that right after you read this chapter you will be able to go out, strap on a kite, and take off, the consequences will not be my responsibility; I disclaim liability for accidents or damage to equipment.

It is just as impossible to learn to fly by reading a book as it is to learn to play the piano without an instrument. But what if you have the instrument, and no teacher?

What I *can* do in this chapter is give you an idea of what to expect from a well run flying school, and give you some basics that will make the instructor's job easier—it is difficult to assimilate detailed theory when the wind is howling in your ear and adrenalin is flowing fast. A well run flying school will not claim to qualify you as a flier as soon as you take lessons. They *will* do everything possible to tell you about the basics affecting your safety and skill. In most cases, $25 to $50 will get you a pretty complete course, sometimes including flights lasting 30 seconds. After that, how you progress is up to you. Some schools will give you your money back if you feel you are not cut out for flying after the first lesson. *All* schools will make you sign a disclaimer for accidents and injuries. They usually supply the kite, harness, and helmet. You will have to supply the boots, gloves, and other clothing.

The first lesson, on the ground, familiarizes you with the various components of the kite, what they do, and how to care for them. Also, you will learn about things such as glide angle, wind effects, and the safety aspects. A film or slide show will give a pretty good idea of what to expect. It is best to join a group of students; they will share their experiences with you, and help you carry the kite up the hill after each flight.

Don't be afraid to ask for the instructor's qualifications. He should stress safety rather than achievement. He should *listen* to your questions, rather than talk incessantly. He should have a written curriculum, assuring you that a thorough course will be taught. The instructor should be sympathetic, yet firm; his advice will help form your flying habits.

If you happen to live too far from the nearest flying school and are absolutely unable to attend one, let this chapter be your guide; but use it along with the advice of an experienced helper. If you attended a flying school, even for a day, you have acquired good, basic skills. Study this chapter carefully, then close your eyes and try to picture yourself in the situations depicted so your every action and reaction becomes second nature to you.

It is a good idea to try on your harness before you go out to a hill. Become accustomed to its feel and make adjustments so that tight straps and buckles won't cut off your circulation. It is also a good idea to fasten a strong beam in a garage or attic from which you can suspend and test the harness. Also, position a crossbar in front of the harness, buckle up, and hang in the air to acquire the feel of being suspended.

If your school has a good site, you won't have to waste time looking for one; but if you are learning by yourself, spare no effort to locate a slope that will enable you to learn safely.

The practice slope should have a rise of about 3:1, its face at an angle of about 20 degrees to the horizontal. You can check this easily with a bubble level and protractor to insure that the glide ratio of your Rogallo wing (4:1) will closely match the space left for gliding. There should be no other slope in front of yours. Most importantly, your practice slope must face *directly into the wind*. There should be no large rocks, trees, or bushes on the slope. Under no circumstances hould you use a cliff or precipice from which to jump and simply "sink or swim." A good slope is smooth, and has fairly loose soil, (plowed earth or sand) to cushion your landings and allow you to slide if necessary.

Having arrived at the site, unload the kite from the car and assemble it carefully. Take your time; you are new to this, and mistakes can be fatal. Make the first assembly near your car where there are tools nearby. Have a helper carry your equipment to the practice site while you carry the kite. So as not to exhaust yourself, get several helpers, if even to just steady a wingtip in the wind.

Find the *exact* direction of the wind. Walk down the slope and tie ribbons to bushes or sticks for an accurate wind indication at every point. The wind should be gentle and steady. If the wind is so strong that you have to struggle with the kite, or so gusty that an unattended kite will be carried aloft suddenly, pack up for the day; this is not the time to make your first flight.

Examine your kite by walking around it, touching every joint and fitting. This inspection tour will save you endless hours of grief. Just recently there was a fatal accident in our area. An *experienced* flier's kite broke up 15 seconds after he took off. A pin was missing from one of the joints on the kite; they found it in his pocket when they carried him away. Please don't let this kind of needless accident happen to you.

Having satisfied yourself that every screw is tight, every pin is in place, the cables are not frayed, and the canvas is not torn, you are ready to don your personal gear. The harness comes first. Tighten all buckles so they will be practically part of your body, yet not so tight that they restrict your circulation. Make sure that none of the webs is crossed, and that the seat is secure. Tighten shoelaces so that your shoes will serve as supports instead of being a nuisance. You should wear fairly heavy boots to prevent twisted ankles. Your shirt should have long sleeves to prevent injuries to your elbows should you land on them. Wear a well fitting helmet that exposes your ears to shouted instructions and the sound of the wind. If it is very cold wear tight, long underwear, not a bulky overcoat or sweater.

Plan a course of action and discuss it with your crew so they can position themselves to assist you. Talking about your

Fig. 6-1. Before attempting to fly, hold the glider and allow its sail to fill with air. (Note the angle of attack.)

flight plan forces you to organize your thoughts and commit them to memory. You may even want to fill out a log book at this point. Have someone with a movie camera record your flight for later reference; do not stand near the top of a long hill for the best lift; stand on the face of the hill where the wind flows parallel to it.

Lift up the kite and buckle yourself in. Make it a habit to buckle the carabiner to the kite as soon as you lift it up. I once saw a fellow make a good run, and leap—only to find he was not hooked up! It could have been disastrous had he taken off from a sheer cliff.

Pick up the nose a little bit. It's a good idea to have a helper whose only job is to hold the tail end of the boom so the nose points slightly upwards. Feel the force of the wind and walk forwards, facing directly into it. Place your hands fairly wide apart on the control bar for good leverage, take a few fast steps, and allow the wind to pick up the kite a little (Fig. 6-1). Do this several times to get a good feel for the effect of the wind on the kite. It will probably feel quite heavy with the wind pushing on it.

Go back up the hill and face the wind again. At an opportune moment, start running down at a moderate pace. following the kite to float in the air *without picking you up* (Fig.

6-2). Try to balance its angle of attack so it goes neither up nor down. After three or four tries, put the kite down with its nose on the ground, facing the wind. Unbuckle, take a deep breath, and sit down. Think about what has happened; discuss it with the others. Do not exert yourself; save your strength. Let others try it for awhile while you relax—as much as you can while you're itching to have another go at it.

The time is here: you are going to learn to fly.

Inspect the kite to make sure it is not damaged, walk up the hill, buckle up, and stand ready with the nose of the kite pointing up slightly. Make flight plans; go over mentally what you are about to do. When the wind is nice and steady, and the kite is well balanced in your hands, start running down the hill directly into the wind. I don't mean start walking, walk fast, or take a few fast hops—I mean run with all the speed you can muster; there is no room for any halfway effort here. (The pilot in Fig. 6-3 knows what I'm talking about.) Just concentrate on running and keep the kite's nose up slightly. After about five steps you will suddenly feel the harness tighten around your thighs. Don't try to jump up or force the kite into the air. Imagine that the kite is trying to latch onto a horizontal rail above it. When you have reached terminal

Fig. 6-2. Buckle yourself in and take a few steps to feel the wind.

Fig. 6-3. At an opportune moment, run; then push the bar out.

velocity—when you simply cannot run any faster—and you are sure that the nose of the kite is pointing upwards correctly, push the control bar away from you about 6 inches. This will make the kite assume a higher angle of attack. Push only for a moment, then immediately pull the bar back to a normal position, closer to your body. If all the conditions are correct, the kite will begin to fly at an angle slightly more gentle than that of the slope itself, and you will be picked up by the harness (Fig. 6-4).

You're flying!—in the air! What a glorious feeling, leaving the ground; even if it is only inches away. For the moment, all you have to do is hold the control bar steady and things will happen by themselves.

As soon as you have the feeling that the harness is holding you up, pull the bar close to you so the angle of attack is less and the kite gains some speed. After about 3 or 4 seconds, let the bar out to a normal position again, settle back, and just relax. But concentrate on the sight, the sound, and the feeling of being in the air.

At first, you will get your "moon legs" (touching the ground every 20 feet or so). Concentrate on keeping your legs and feet together and your body relaxed. Most beginners windmill their legs through the air during their first flight.

This tends to upset the balance of the kite and makes the pilot prone to landing injuries.

When you see the ground rush up to your feet, simply push the bar away from you and towards the wind. Remember what your wind indicators told you on the ground. The kite should flare out, slow down, and settle in a nice, standup landing. (See Fig. 6-5 for the sequence described.)

Regardless of the kind of landing you made, you will be exhilarated. Catch your breath, place the kite on the ground, nose down and pointing into the wind, and unbuckle. Sit under the kite and consider all that has transpired. If the landing was rough, try to figure out what went wrong.

There are two basic mistakes beginners make when learning to fly Rogallo wings. The first is that they try to coax the kite into the air, either by jumping up or by pushing the control bar forward too soon before flying speed has been reached. If the bar is pushed forward prematurely, the kite will present itself to the wind like a sail. The tremendous air pressure exerted, instead of lifting you, will only make the kite rear up. The pilot will be lifted in the air, but instead of flying he will merely dangle there for a second or two, the tail of the kite will hit the ground, and the flier will settle with it. In a severe case, the wind will flip the kite, with the pilot still buckled in. Fortunately, this very seldom happens.

Fig. 6-4. Once your feet leave the ground, pull the bar in to fly.

117

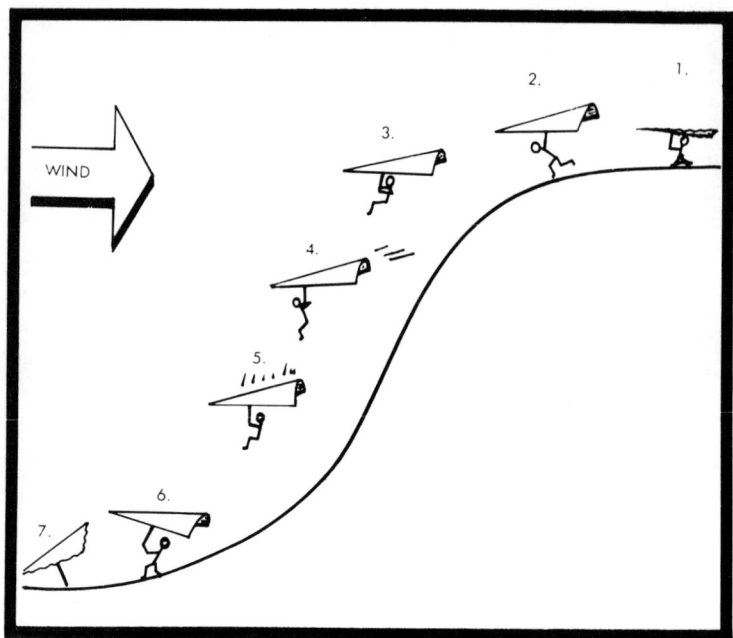

Fig. 6-5. The basic flight sequence: (1) Think ahead and buckle yourself in; (2) run as fast as you can, pushing the bar out; (3) pull the bar in and settle down to fly; (4) pull the bar in to gain speed and prevent stalls; (5) push the bar out to slow down; (6) when close to the ground, push the bar out even more, and flare-out into a standup landing position; and (7) immediately after landing put the nose of the kite down.

The second mistake is that of the pilot who does not push the bar away at the right moment, or does so when his flying speed is insufficient. In this case, the kite will follow the slope angle of the hill and gradually settle to the ground. The strapped-in pilot, unwilling (or unable) to let go of the bar, will be dragged along on his stomach. This usually does not cause any damage—other than to the flier's ego. Clearly, he should have waited for more wind, run faster, been on a steeper slope, or pushed the bar out sooner and farther.

When you have reached the "moon leg" stage there is not much else to do except repeat the experience. Two things should be said in favor of learning to fly hang gliders. One can learn a stage at a time; and one need only go beyond a stage when he feels competent enough to do so. Repeat your flights, starting from the same point, until you are able to repeat every stage several times without failure. Only in this manner can you gain the skill and confidence that comes with a conscious, preplanned action.

If, in spite of your best efforts, the kite seems unable to lift you, or continues to stall without flying smoothly, there may be something wrong with the center of gravity. You should try attaching your harness to the keel at a point nearer the rear end. If the kite keeps stalling, attach the harness closer to the nose. In either case, make sure that there is sufficient room between you and the control bar to enable full control of the kite. To control the kite, you will move the control bar to change the angle of the sail. If the control bar is too close to your body, you might not be able to pull it in close enough to gain speed when you need it. On the other hand, the bar must not be too far away; you have to reach it to cause a gentle stall for landing.

You may make your first hops at the bottom of the hill or a few feet up the slope. After several successful hops you can progress to a starting point 15 feet higher. Higher on the hill, you will find that some flights will be longer than others. This is because of wind changes and inconsistencies in your technique. Repeat the starting procedure faithfully. Have your assistant run along to steady the kite, but don't let him actually push it. *You* must provide the speed. In this regard, it would be beneficial to embark on a physical fitness program before you begin to take flying lessons. Carrying a 40-pound kite up and down a hill all day, and slipping and sliding in the sand, is exhausting if you are not in good shape. Jogging and weight lifting are good tuneup exercises for hang gliding.

Hang gliders a few years ago had two bars parallel to the direction of flight, from which the pilot hung during his flight. Today, the trapeze bar is almost universally used. Advanced fliers use a prone harness which permits them to fly in the horizontal position (Fig. 6-6). This cuts down on wind resistance and increases the glide angle.

Your initial flights should be in a straight line; it is of utmost importance to correct for any turning tendencies caused by a shift in the wind or in your center of gravity. If you

Fig. 6-6. The ultimate high—flying prone.

drift from this line, simply pull yourself towards it. This will dip the wingtip on the side towards the line, and will force the kite to resume its course. You may have to pull until you land. To cushion your landing keep the bar to one side and simply push it away from you (Fig. 6-7). Immediately after your feet touch the ground, pull the nose of the kite down; otherwise, the kite might flip over backwards. Keep the nose on the ground for a few seconds, then unbuckle. If the kite lifts up, it could carry you with it. When this happens, you have to unbuckle the harness immediately, run to the front, hang onto the front flying wires, and pull the kite to the ground with all your strength.

If you plan another flight immediately afterwards, do not be afraid to ask someone to help you carry the kite up the hill again (Fig. 6-8). Arriving at the top, completely exhausted, heart beating, and knees trembling, you are in no condition to execute a coordinated takeoff procedure (Fig. 6-9). In fact, you run the risk of taking off wobbly-kneed in a crosswind direction which may have disastrous consequences.

In general, learning to fly should be a pleasant experience. Don't rush it. Laugh at your mistakes and analyze them; don't "see red" and make the same mistake again. Always stress safety above anything else. If the kite is bent or damaged, repair it. If there is a question about its reparability at the site, call it a day and do the job right, at home; there will be many more days of flying ahead, *if* your equipment is in good shape.

Fig. 6-7. Note the extremely high altitude of the kite's nose upon landing.

Fig. 6-8. Have your helpers carry the kite up the hill again.

Soon the day will come when you will experience enough lift to be able to make a slight turn. Examining the basics of hang gliding, it is easy to see that the pilot hangs from the harness like a pendulum, more or less vertically, regardless of what the kite does. The kite is light; the pilot, heavy. When he pulls the kite one way, the kite's angle of attack changes, but

Fig. 6-9. If you are alone, this is the proper way to carry a kite.

the pilot continues hanging vertically. Once this is realized, the control movements become reflex.

Simply put, to turn the kite pull the control bar towards you, and the side to which you want to turn. Some pilots find this difficult to learn and waste a lot of time trying to figure it out in the air, resulting in delays and unsatisfactory progress. In fact, unless the basics become reflex, the pilot may panic and lose control later in his course.

Turn the nose only about 30 degrees from the flight path. Remember, when the kite is sideways it presents a large area to the wind and may get carried towards the hill, against your intentions. A 30-degree change in course, combined with your forward speed and the wind coming up the hill, will result in a flight path somewhat parallel to the hill. After a few seconds, execute a turn in the opposite direction to drift back towards the usual landing area. The "turn in the opposite direction" is actually only a 90-degree turn (Fig. 6-10) which will put you on a course going back towards the starting point. You should *never* try 180-degree turns—they will send you back towards the hill! This can be serious. If the wind ever turns you towards the hill, your flight speed will add to the wind speed, lift will be lost, and you will land at about 30 mph—hard!

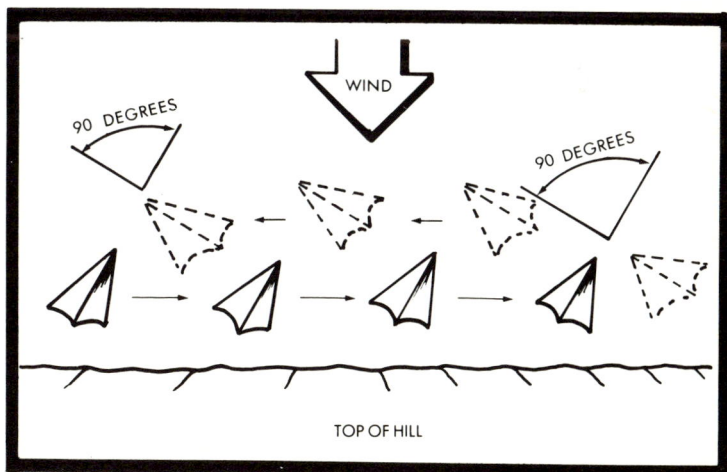

Fig. 6-10. When soaring over a ridge, "quarter" into the wind (crisscross it). Make 90-degree turns to reverse the flight path.

Fig. 6-11. Flying like a bird—in ridge lift!

Unless you're hundreds of feet in the air, don't ever **turn towards the hill**. Make gentle turns so the kite crisscrosses the wind and skims over the slope parallel to the hill. When this technique is acquired, you will be able to soar back and forth over the same spot for a long time (Fig. 6-11). It is important to realize that when the kite is banked, as in a turn, the stall speed will increase. If you are close to stalling and suddenly enter a turn, you will stall completely. Gain some speed before entering a turn. Not only will your control be more positive, but dangerous stalls will be prevented.

Once in a while you will encounter sudden lift; the wind may pick up, or you may fly over a ridge or thermal-producing area (such as a blacktop road). Don't overreact. See if the kite will regain its balance without having to touch the control bar. Apply corrections sparingly; chances are the lift is local in nature and your pendulum position will pull the kite back to the correct attitude.

If you have enough altitude, 360-degree turns can be made relatively easily. Complete turnarounds must not be attempted unless you are at least 500 feet high and the wind is steady. The kite loses altitude very rapidly in a turn. Its glide ratio may go as low as 1:1, something the inexperienced flier wouldn't anticipate. In general, a 360-degree turn is considered an advanced flying maneuver to be taught by an experienced instructor.

124

If you wish to take advantage of good lift, it is best to trim the kite for minimum sink speed. This can be achieved with a high angle of attack. With a high angle of attack, the kite will fly very slowly, and forward speed will be slow; at the same time, the controls will be sluggish and the kite will be "mushy." A stall must be watched for every second.

On the other hand, if you wish to fly a long distance, pull the control bar in. This places the center of gravity forwards causing the kite to fly fast. Speed can often spare you some disasters. If you are preparing to land, and spot a barbed wire fence just ahead, you might not be sure of what to do; should you mush it in, or what? The best course, in this case, is to make the kite glide fast—even if it looks like you're heading straight for the fence! Why? Because a fast flying kite is easier to control. Even under the worst of circumstances it can be made to zoom over the obstacle in the last second. A slow flying kite would stall if you tried the same maneuver. Contrary to popular belief, it is actually dangerous to fly low, or slowly. Height gives you time to think, room to maneuver. Speed gives you control.

Listen to the sounds of your kite in the air. If the kite suddenly goes quiet, it may mean an impending stall. If it makes excessive noise, you may be flying dangerously fast. Your ears must not be covered. If necessary, drill some earholes in the helmet. Get used to the sounds of your kite: the flapping of the canvas; the hum of the wires; the sounds associated with proper flying speeds.

Approaching a landing you will find that just before touching the ground there will be sudden additional lift. This is due to the *ground effect*: the interaction between the downwash of the wings and the ground. The ground effect helps you "flare out" the landing. To land properly, skim so low over the gound that you actually have to pull your feet up, then swoop up to create additional lift. Success is a completely stalled, standup landing.

Some gliders have seating arrangements for a passenger. Obviously, a tremendous amount of lift is needed to lift two people. The inertia and momentum of their weight must be compensated for by the judicious application of control movements. Experts, such as Bob Wills, have taken passengers aloft at Torrey Pines, near San Diego, California. There, however, the ridge lift is often so powerful that even with two people on board, additional helpers have to hold the kite down until the moment of launching.

Although most hang gliders are launched by the pilot from slopes or cliffs, successful attempts have been made at launching by other means. Bill Bennett and others have flown in the winter by donning skis and sliding down a snowy slope to gain flying speed. The technique is almost normal, although cold winds and gusty conditions present additional problems. Some enterprising pilots actually tie their hang gliders to the gondolas of hot-air balloons. When the balloon reaches the proper altitude, the kite is released. Since the kite's wings immediately fill with air, it glides quite comfortably to the ground.

It is also possible to foot-launch a hang glider by attaching a rope to it and having two helpers run into the wind pulling it. This is potentially dangerous because of the possibility that the structure will fail, the tow rope doesn't detach at the right moment, or the pilot may be inexperienced in this kind of launching. Some kites are towed behind boats. The tremendous pull of the rope must be borne by a strong, steel trapeze bar. When the kite reaches the proper altitude, the rope is detached and free flight begins. Soaring is usually impossible because there is little lift over water. The rope-release device must work every time, and the flier must wear a special harness which can be detached from the kite at a moment's notice to drop him in the water, should the landing be unsuccessful. The kite must be equipped with some flotation gear, such as Styrofoam blocks at the wingtips and trapeze bar; and the pilot should wear a life jacket. Flying over water is dangerous because when the kite lands, the wave motion acting on the huge sail may destroy the kite frame. It is best not to fight a water-logged kite; a man's strength is hardly ever sufficient to offset Nature's forces.

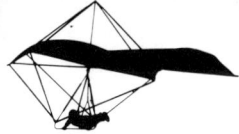

Chapter 7

Meteorology

When one takes lessons in scuba diving, one of the subjects discussed is water; of course. Since one swims in water, it is appropriate to discuss water: how much it weighs, how it flows, and how it can be dangerous. So it is with hang gliding. We fly our gliders, relying on air to hold us up. It's only appropriate to discuss air and its movements.

In early days of hang gliding, the simple rule was: face the wind and fly only as high as you would care to fall. Modern hang gliding takes place much higher up than most people care to fall. In fact, we are fast approaching the day when we will challenge the clouds.

It may come as a surprise to many readers that air has weight. Air, a combination of gases, is made up of molecules which have weight. It has been determined that at 32°F and at sea level, there are 6.03×10^{23} molecules in 22.4 liters of air (about 5½ gallons). That's alot of molecules—a number derived by writing twenty-three 10's and connecting them with multiplication signs! By careful measurement, scientists have determined that a cubic foot of air weighs about 0.075 lb (at sea level). This may not seem like much until you consider a large volume, such as a room or the airspace above a town. In a large volume air may weigh tons. Air is a lot less dense than water, but behaves in a somewhat similar manner; with one exception: air is compressible. The more it is compressed, the more it weighs per unit of volume. A simple gas-compression device is a tire pump. By compressing air with the pump until it overcomes the pressure on a tire valve, it is possible to

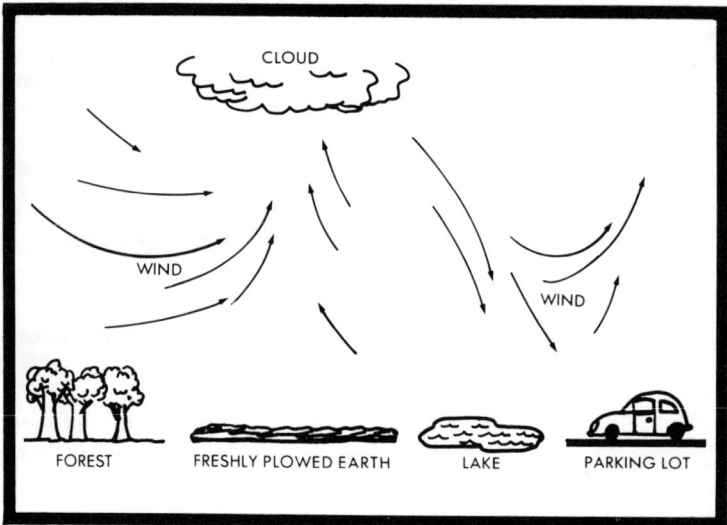

Fig. 7-1. How wind is generated over hot and cold surfaces.

amass so much air in the tire that the molecules are very close together and exert a large force on the walls of the tire. We say that the tire has pressure in it. It is also possible to raise the pressure of air by heating it. When a gas is cooled, its pressure is decreased because the molecules do not race around with as much vigor as before. When a gas is heated in an open space, its molecules collide with greater force and compel each other to take up more space. In other words, when air is heated, it expands to a larger volume. Since a certain amount of air has a constant weight, when its volume becomes larger, its density becomes less. Heavier, surrounding air tries to get under lighter air to push it up. As the light air moves upwards, the space it occupied is gradually filled with colder, denser air from the side. This air movement is called wind (Fig. 7-1). Whenever we feel wind, it is rushing towards a spot which has recently been heated.

When the air near the surface of the earth becomes heated **and rises, it takes moisture with it.** When it reaches a height where the surrounding temperature is colder, the moisture precipitates and becomes visible: a cloud is formed. Clouds formed by rising hot air usually grow quite fast and if they cannot support more moisture, it will rain.

Certain parts of the earth absorb the sun's rays more readily than others and, therefore, radiate more heat than other areas. As the wind sweeps across the countryside, it picks up heat from freshly plowed fields where the black earth radiates heat. Heat is also radiated by flat rocks and dark parking lots. The air suddenly expands and rises above areas such as these. The rising "bubbles" of air are called *thermals*. They may or may not terminate in a cloud. There are some relatively cold areas over which the moving air loses its heat and moves downwards. A lush forest, for example, is relatively cooler than a parking lot; the vertical air movement is downwards over a forest.

As one flies through a thermal one becomes immersed in it, and moves with it. If the air movement differentials are quite radical, an airplane would bounce up or down violently. This phenomenon is commonly referred to as "air pockets." If the airplane flies through a rising current of air whose upward speed is the same as the sink speed of the plane, the airplane will neither sink nor gain elevation. This is called a *zero sink condition*. If the air rises faster than the sink speed of the plane, the pilot will gain altitude. If the sink speed of the plane is 8 ft/sec and the thermal rises at 10 ft/sec, the plane will gain altitude at 2 ft/sec in the thermal. Similarly, if the air movement is downwards, its sink speed will add to the sink speed of the plane.

The actual appearance of a thermal, if we could see it, would be much like a puff of smoke going upwards. At first, the puff would be quite small, then it would grow bigger on top and become quite high. The bottom of it may break loose from the earth; the thermal would act much like a huge ball rising upwards (Fig. 7-2). Below the thermal, cool air rushes in to take its place. The thermal rises upwards until it reaches a cool layer where it dissipates. Because of these effects, when one glider is in a thermal, another glider just a few hundred feet below may not experience any lift at all. The actual circumference of a thermal may vary from a few feet to a few hundred feet. Thus, to stay in the rising bubble of air, the pilot must circle several times. When one flies a thermal, one must turn left, and then turn right quickly to "map" the extent and

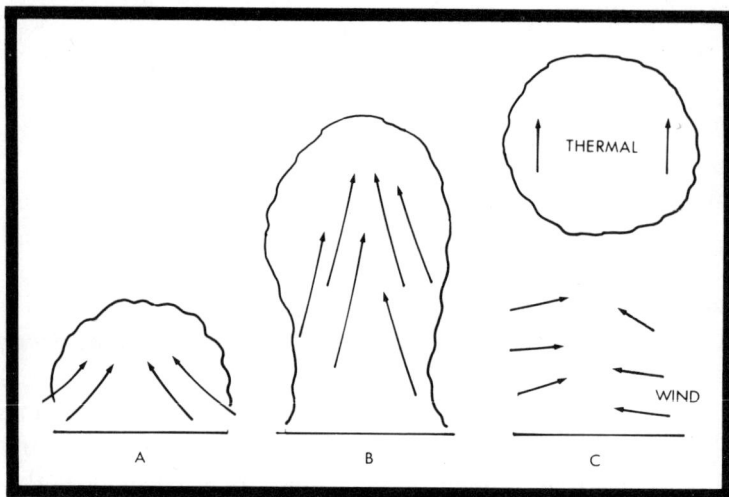

Fig. 7-2. Three stages in the formation of a thermal.

location of the thermal. If the wind is steady, somewhere downwind there must be an area where air is being heated and replaced by cooler air. The wind, as it sweeps over the land, flows around and over obstacles in its path. When it encounters a billboard, it flows around the front of it and swirls behind it where it causes vortexes (Fig. 7-3). The front of the billboard

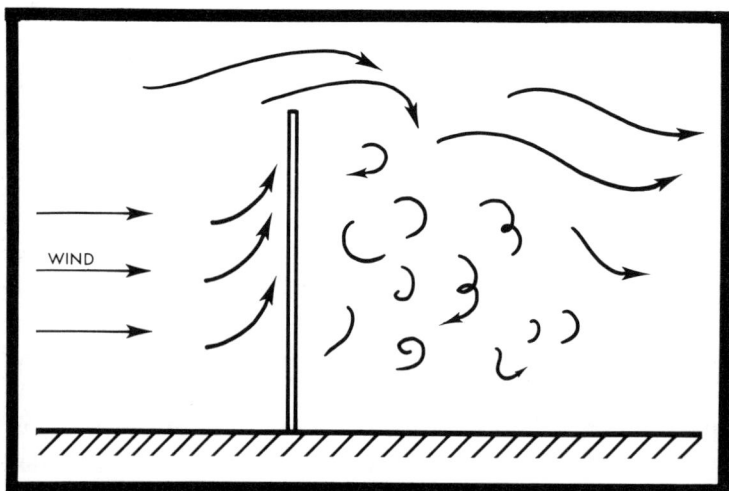

Fig. 7-3. When moving air strikes an obstacle, a vortex is formed behind the obstacle.

will be a high pressure area; the rear, a low pressure area. If the obstacle is not at a right angle to the wind, but at a lesser one, the air molecules will move across the face of it smoothly. For instance, a smooth hillside will force the air to move over it, and parallel to it. Since the air moves upwards, it may provide enough lift to allow a hang glider to stay up for extended periods. When the air mass reaches the top of the hill, its mass compels it to keep moving in the same direction. This means that there will be an area of low pressure and turbulence directly behind the brow of the hill. This is commonly called the *rotor* (Fig. 7-4). The air movement in this area is downwards and unpredictable. Hang gliders should stay away from rotors; they spell danger! Several horizontal ridges or bumps on a hill will cause their own rotors to form.

Because air has weight, it obeys the laws of gravity. If a hill in the path of the wind is small, the air will try to flow around it, rather than climb over it. Similarly, if the hill has a jutting edge (Fig. 7-5) it will cleave the air mass, causing it to

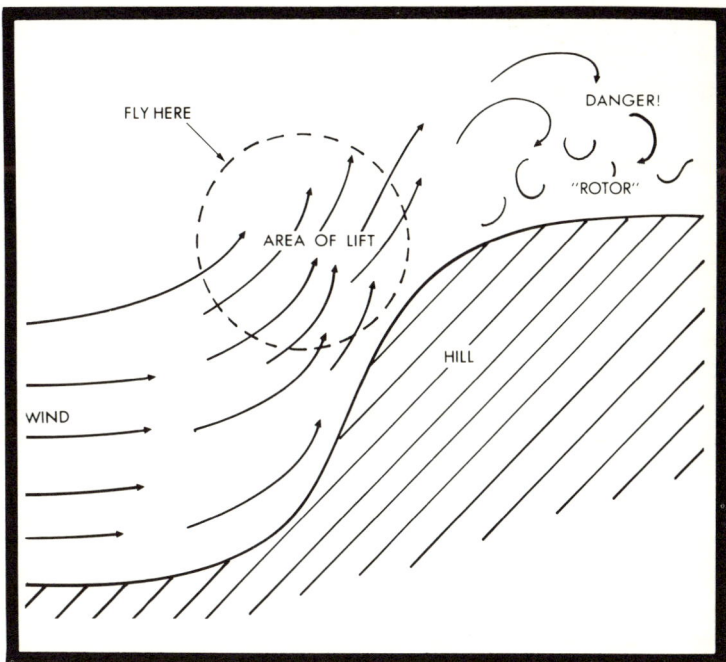

Fig. 7-4. Ridge lift results when wind strikes the face of a hill.

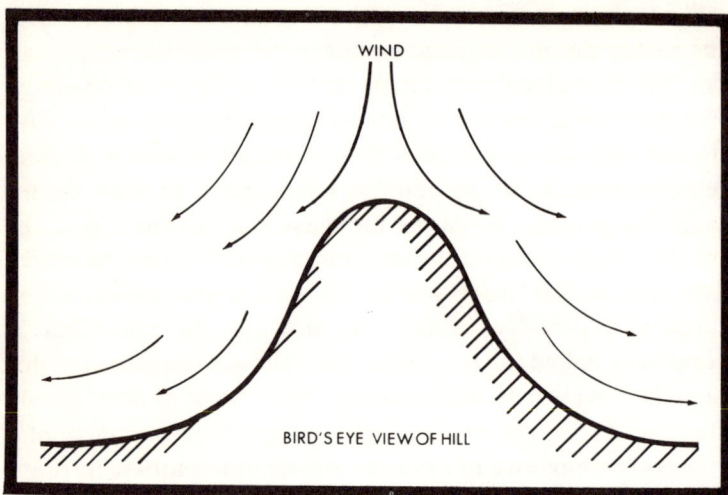

Fig. 7-5. Jutting tongues of a hill make the wind divide, but do not cause it to move upwards.

separate. In this case, the air will flow more or less horizontally on either side of the jutting land mass. There will be very little upward movement of air in such an area and hang gliders would not experience extended periods of sufficient lift there. On the other hand, if there is a valley or crevice on the front side of the hill, the air movement will compress the molecules and the higher pressure will force the air upwards. Thus, there is always lift at the very center of crevices which face the wind. Only large, bowl-shaped valleys have sufficient air space to provide room for flying. At the point where the walls of the bowl join the face of the hill, there is only horizontal air movement because the wind is merely trying to find the easiest way around the hill (Fig. 7-6).

Only by careful study and observation can one acquire the skill necessary to take advantage of air movements. Birds have an instinct for finding lift. Pilots should make it a habit to observe them; where birds circle, there is bound to be lift. Seagulls are often seen flying back and forth in front of the face of a hill, an excellent sign that cliff flying will be good for hang gliders too.

Flying over a cliff can have its problems. Air is compressed in front of a hill. Thus, the layer of air immediately next to the hill moves slower than air just a few feet farther away. This may mean control problems when you turn and the hang glider is banked.

Since the earth warms up during the day, it is usually warmer near the ground than it is in the air. Several scientific measurements have proven that the air temperature drops about 1 degree for every 180 feet of rise in altitude. This is called the *lapse rate*. When air is forced over the face of a hill, it develops momentum; it tends to continue upwards. This is helped by the lapse rate because as the air begins to move upwards, it acts like a hot air bubble buoyed up by surrounding cold air. The warm bubble of air may soar skywards for hundreds of feet, way past the brow of the hill.

Another cause of rising air is the difference in temperatures between two large masses of air. For instance, if a cold storm front meets a hot prevailing air mass, the cold air will slide under the hot air. This automatically lifts the hot air. If a glider happens into the hot air mass, it too will be lifted. It takes a great deal of experience to detect lift in such areas. Lift due to differences in air temperatures is called *shear lift*; it has been known to carry gliders skywards for hundreds of feet.

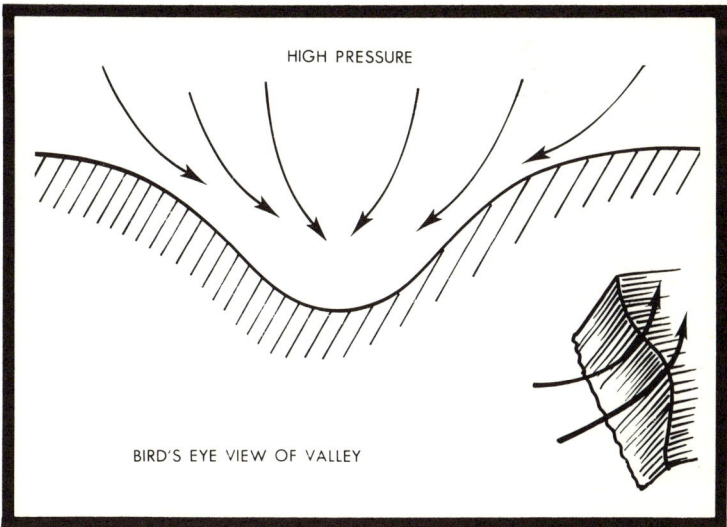

Fig. 7-6. High pressure, and lift, is created by wind in a valley.

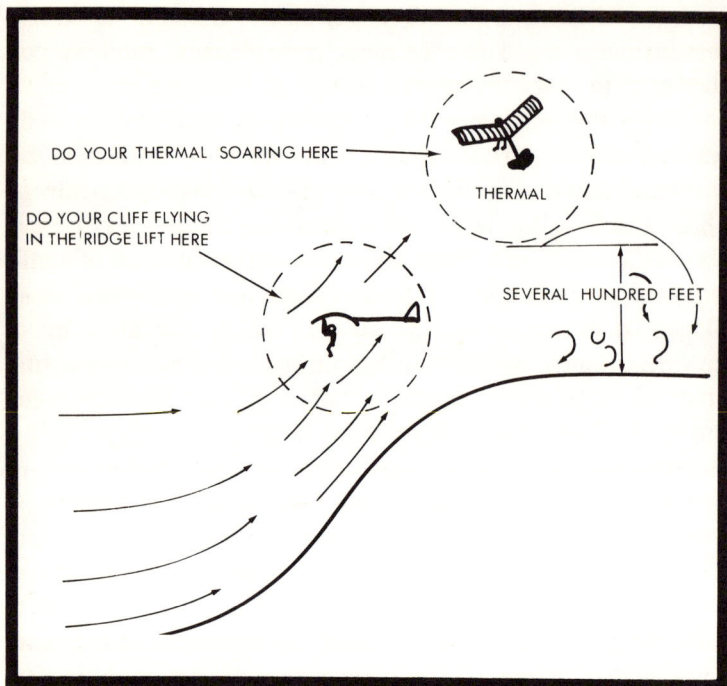

Fig. 7-7. The ideal spot for ridge flying is over the brow of a hill.

The so-called *environmental lapse rate* (ELR) is the measure of the differences between the temperatures of the various layers of air. The *adiabatic lapse rate* (ALR) is that of a cooling bubble of air. Thus, the ELR is stated in degrees Fahrenheit per foot of altitude; the ALR, in degrees Fahrenheit per minute. A rising bubble of air has a certain temperature and moisture content different from that of the surrounding atmosphere. Cooling is also affected by expansion caused by lower pressures the bubble encounters moving upwards. When the ELR exceeds the ALR an unstable condition occurs that makes the bubble of air continue to rise. In the reverse case, the bubble of air remains stable in altitude and quickly dissipates.

If you ever travel to a faraway flying spot, ask the local inhabitants about prevailing wind conditions and any signs of an atmospheric disturbance. For instance, in one Southern California area, the wind always seems to pick up around 3 p.m. Its direction is directly inland from the ocean. In rocky, mountainous areas the weather may change suddenly; a shower may start any minute and be over just as quickly. To prepare for changing wind and weather conditions, consult weather charts. Areas of equal pressure are connected by curves on the charts. Having your own wind velocity meter, barometer, and wind direction indicator (windsock), is a good way to "play it safe." Marking the weather conditions in the log book also helps one to keep up with changing wind conditions in any location. During a contest, for instance, it may come in handy to know that at that particular flying site the wind picks up at a certain time of day, or that the wind comes in gusts every 10 seconds. Delaying your start may mean the difference between winning and crashing.

Some clubs and individuals have developed a system of weather reporting whereby cooperative, local farmers are phoned about flying conditions. A wind direction and speed indicator is installed on the farmer's house at the club's expense; the farmer simply reports the numbers indicated on the meters. Correlating this information with information on ideal flying days, it is easy to judge the suitability of the wind for any given day.

Local newspapers are also good sources of weather information. You can learn to correlate their weather reports with actual flying conditions. For instance, if *The Los Angeles Times* reports the wind to be between 12 and 20 knots from a direction between northwest and southwest in the San Diego area, it means that flying will be great at the Torrey Pines Cliffs from noon until sundown.

Chapter 8

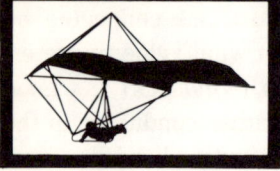

Tools of the Trade

Any sport or hobby which involves the use of mechanical equipment also necessitates the use of tools. Because hang gliders are made up of mechanical parts like nuts, screws, bolts, and turnbuckles, it is necessary to have at least an elementary set of tools.

Some hang gliders are manufactured so that the user does not have to have tools to assemble them. But many kites have bolts and nuts that have to be loosened and tightened for assembly, disassembly, and tuning as well. It is impossible to tighten aircraft locknuts without a wrench. There are several types of wrenches which can be used (Fig. 8-1).

The open-end wrench usually has a long handle, at either end of which is a U-shaped opening. One end of the wrench is

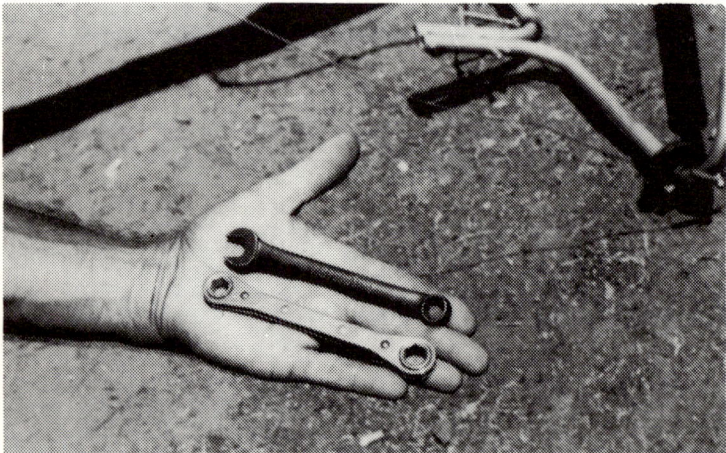

Fig. 8-1. The two most popular wrenches used by hang glider pilots.

larger than the other to accommodate two nuts of different sizes. The size of the nut, measured across its flat faces, is stamped on the face of each corresponding wrench opening. You can learn to judge the size of nuts with a little practice. Always use the proper wrench; a wrench which is too large will round out the corners of the nut and make it useless. Foreign-made screws have threads which are sized materially. They require metric wrenches. Some wrenches completely encircle the nut. These are the best because they put pressure on all corners of the nut evenly. There are closed-end wrenches with built-in ratcheting devices which make it possible to loosen or tighten nuts with back and forth action only (Fig. 8-2). These wrenches are very popular with hang glider pilots. You will find that pilots carry their favorite wrenches attached to their belts, ready for use after each landing.

There are also wrenches which can be adjusted for a wide range of nut sizes by simply turning a serrated screw. Use adjustable wrenches in an emergency only; their jaws, seldom parallel, may damage the nuts.

A pair of pliers is very handy to have. Pliers can have long slender jaws for holding and bending wire. Some combination

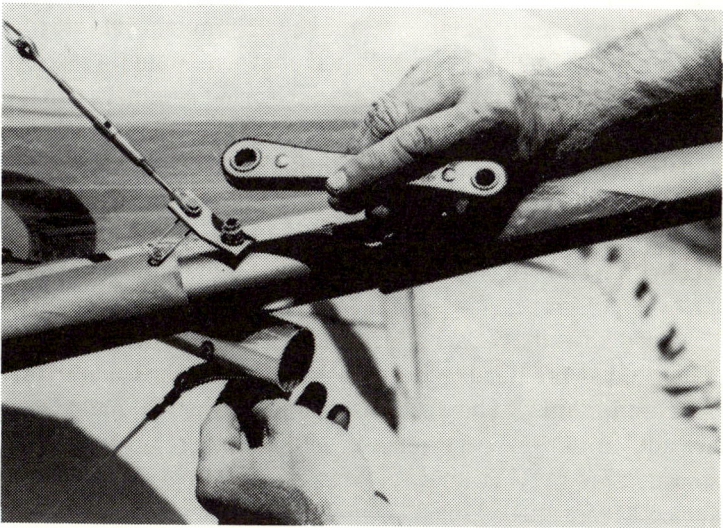

Fig. 8-2. Ratchet wrenches are fast and convenient to use.

pliers have serrated jaws for holding and two wire-cutting edges on the side. Never use pliers to tighten or loosen a nut.

Screwdrivers may also be needed. Some have a flat blade to fit slotted screws. Use the proper size blade for each screw. Most needs can be satisfied with a blade about ¼ inch wide. There are other types of blades made for special screws, such as the cross-shaped blade of the Phillips screwdriver. Some hang gliders are made with Allen-head bolts. These bolts, with a hexagon-shaped recess in the head, have to be tightened with an L-shaped key whose cross section is also hexagonal.

A basic toolkit should be carried in the accessory bag of any hang glider. On-the-spot repairs can mean the difference between a spoiled day and successful flights. If you wish to perform major repairs or build your own hang glider, a well equipped home workshop is a necessity. Some kites have been fabricated in bedrooms, but it is best to work in a shop where some dirt on the floor and a general mess can be tolerated once in awhile.

The most popular workshop is usually the garage. A workbench can be set up, and the large, flat floor can be used for the important lining-up operations. Make sure there is ample light, and the floor is level and smooth. Paint the walls a bright, light color. Install a good overhead light in the middle of the work area. You can make a simple, yet sturdy workbench from 2 by 4's and ¾-inch plywood. Mount a vise on one corner of the workbench. Hooks or spring retainers can be mounted on a vertical surface (or pegboard) to serve as tool holders. In general, the neater the area is kept, the more pleasure you will have working there; and as a rule, the neater the job will be. A well equipped workshop contains many tools, each with a specific application (Fig. 8-3). Let us discuss them one by one.

Wood saws have large teeth, as a rule. The wood saw is seldom used for hang gliders because most parts are made from aluminum. If you are constructing a wooden glider, ask the advice of an experienced cabinetmaker or precision carpenter as to what kinds of saws to buy. The saw used for cutting across the grain of wood is different from that used to cut parallel to the grain. Plywood and veneers require

Fig. 8-3. A well equipped workshop makes it easy to build kites.

fine-tooth saws. Special hacksaws are available for cutting aluminum. In general, the thinner the material to be cut, the more teeth per inch the saw blade should have. When you cut across thin sections of aluminum, make sure that at least three teeth are always in contact with the material. Failing to do this will cause the saw blade to jump, the teeth to chip, and the cut

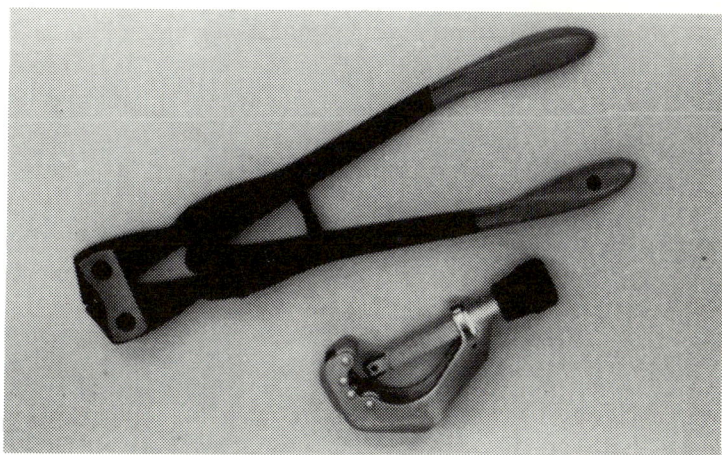

Fig. 8-4. Tube cutter (bottom) and cable cutting tool.

to be irregular. How do you put three teeth in contact with $^1/_{16}$-inch sheet metal? Simply hold the saw blade at an angle to the metal so it cuts diagonally instead of straight acloss. To cut aluminum tubes with a saw, the tube has to be held securely, either by a helper or by the suitably padded jaws of a vise. If a pipe wrench is used, make sure that its jaws are properly padded to distribute the load over the aluminum.

It is difficult to cut aluminum tubing without collapsing it. Professionals avoid this difficulty by using a curved tool (looking somewhat like a C-clamp) with a hard, sharp roller in it. To cut a tube, place the tube in the crook of the tool, gently tighten the roller around the tube by turning the handle, and rotate the cutter around the tube. After each complete revolution, the handle is tightened slightly. Usually it takes about four complete revolutions to cut thin-wall tubing in two.

Placing a cross bolt in an aluminum tube either collapses the tube or wears out the hole rapidly, unless adequate precautions are taken. It is best to place a wood dowel in the tube at the appropriate location, drill an oversize hole, and insert a metal bushing in the hole. A flat-head screw is then placed at either end of the tube (Fig. 8-5) and a hammer is used to drive it in. This peens the ends of the bushing over the hole. The flat-head screws are removed, and the bushing is ready to accept the cross bolt.

Bending aluminum tubes takes a bit of experience. One method is to place a close-fitting metal spring around the tube where the bend is to be made. The best method is to use a tube-bending tool that provides lateral support at both sides of the bend. Without support, the tube will buckle and become weak. Remember, even properly executed bends stretch the outside fibers of the pipe; you may stress it beyond the yield point. After each bending operation, inspect the tube for cracks or signs of stretching. Lacking the tools necessary to prevent overstressing the tube, you can simply fill the tube with fine sand, tramped down hard, before you proceed with the bending operation.

Drills are needed to make holes in aluminum or steel parts. The drill is comprised of two parts: the hand drill, either hand-cranked or motor-driven, and the drill bit. Drill bits come

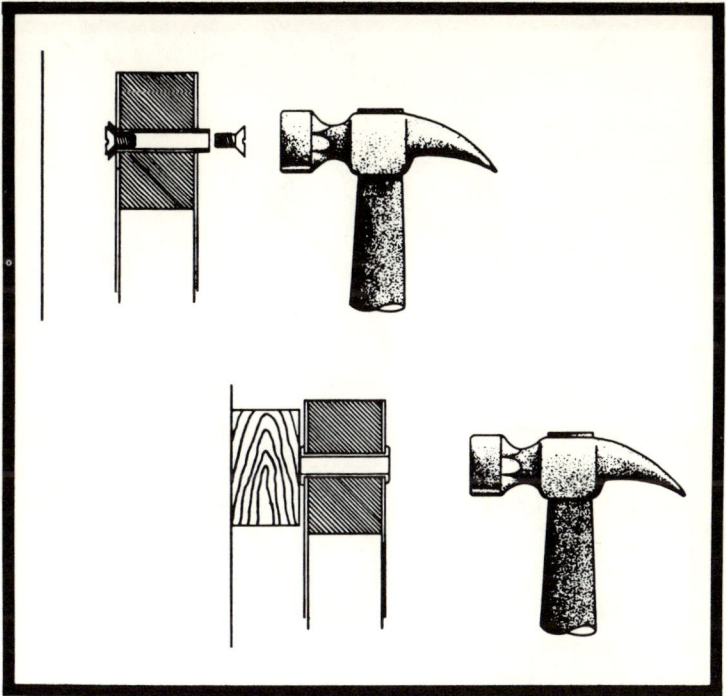

Fig. 8-5. Bushing the bolt holes. (Courtesy Manta Products)

in many sizes and care must be taken to use the correct one. Keep the bits properly sharpened, and in their proper holders. Hold the part to be drilled securely so it doesn't "climb up" on the bit when it breaks through. When drilling sheet metal, it may help to place a piece of wood on top of the metal and clamp the whole thing to the drill table. This prevents the metal from being chewed up.

Before a hole is drilled, its location must be marked. Use a pointed scribe (or nail) to scratch a couple of lines that intersect at the exact center of the hole. It is always the center of the hole that is measured from another location—e.g., the end of the tube, or the edge of a plate. When you are satisfied that the location is correct, make an indentation at the intersection with a center punch. This is a tool whose hard, sharp point is placed at the cross, and the other end tapped smartly with a hammer. The indentation makes it easy to hold the drill bit in place when you start the hole.

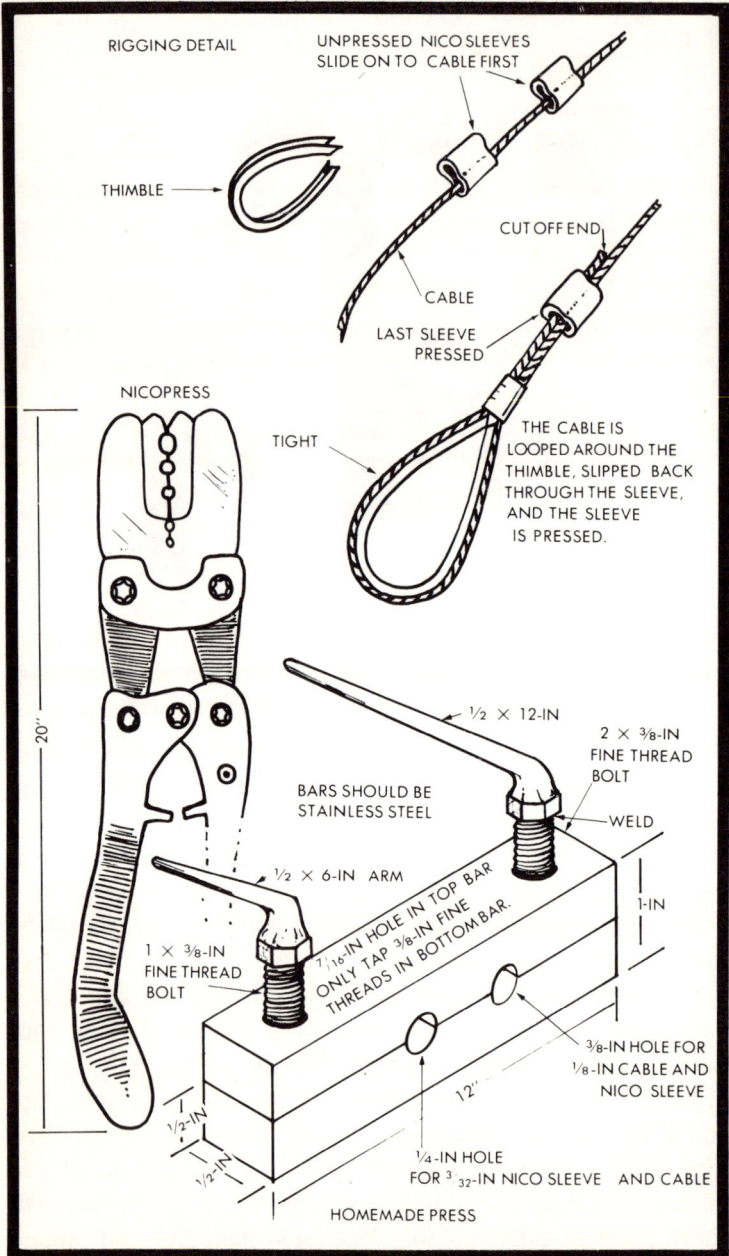

RIGGING DETAIL

THIMBLE

UNPRESSED NICO SLEEVES
SLIDE ON TO CABLE FIRST

CABLE

CUT OFF END

LAST SLEEVE
PRESSED

NICOPRESS

TIGHT

THE CABLE IS
LOOPED AROUND THE
THIMBLE, SLIPPED BACK
THROUGH THE SLEEVE,
AND THE SLEEVE
IS PRESSED.

20"

½ × 12-IN

2 × ⅜-IN
FINE THREAD
BOLT

WELD

BARS SHOULD BE
STAINLESS STEEL

½ × 6-IN ARM

1 × ⅜-IN
FINE THREAD
BOLT

7/16-IN HOLE IN TOP BAR
ONLY TAP ⅜-IN FINE
THREADS IN BOTTOM BAR.

1-IN

⅜-IN HOLE FOR
⅛-IN CABLE AND
NICO SLEEVE

½-IN

½-IN

12"

¼-IN HOLE
FOR 3/32-IN NICO SLEEVE AND CABLE

HOMEMADE PRESS

Fig. 8-6. The Nicopress and its homemade counterpart. (Courtesy
Whitney Enterprises)

It is always a good policy to use a small drill first, and then graduate to the final size. Large drills—anything over $^3/_{16}$ inch—have a center flute which pushes the metal. The small starting drill is used to make a hole large enough for the center flute on a larger drill to rotate, unimpeded, while its outside cutting edge makes a larger hole. Practice drilling scrap pieces before proceeding with the actual work. If two or more pieces have to be accurately aligned for drilling, clamp them together. It is particularly difficult to make a hole right across the centerline of a rod or tube. If the hole is off center, one side of the metal will be weaker than the other. A *drill jig* must be used when drilling cross holes. Even a block of hardwood will do a respectable job of locating holes across a tube. If several tubes have to be drilled, make a drill-jig block with hardened bushings to guide the drill bit across the centerline.

Wire cables are used extensively in the construction of hang gliders. The safest method of attaching cable is to curl the cable's end around a *thimble* and then secure it with a Nicopress sleeve. You can use a large Nicopress tool (quite expensive) for this purpose, or you can crimp the sleeves with a homemade version (Fig. 8-6). Swage-It, a tool manufactured by the S&F Tool Co., 1245 Logan Ave., Costa Mesa, CA 92626, costs about $12 and only a wrench is needed to press its two jaws together (Fig. 8-7). Again, experiment with scrap pieces before you trust your life to a homemade cable joint.

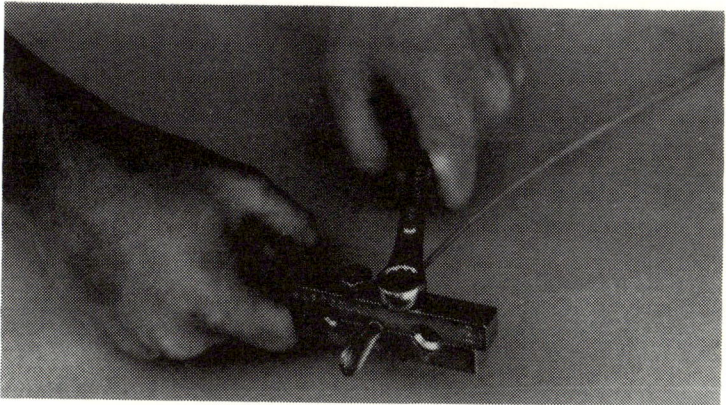

Fig. 8-7. Swaging tool manufactured by S&F Tool Co.

The sail cloth used for the wings must be sewn on a heavy-duty machine capable of zig-zag stitching. Lay the cloth on the floor and measure the panels carefully before you cut. Use pinking shears to avoid fraying. When the cloth panels are perfectly aligned, with a slight overlap, join them with tape that is sticky on both sides. The tape, Seamstik, locates the cloth securely during the sewing operations. Have several helpers give you a hand if you do your own sewing. A seam ripper can be used on seams which are less than perfect. If several layers of cloth have to be sewn together, and the machine is not capable of handling it, a hand awl may be used.

Attachment points for cloth can be reinforced with brass grommets. First, the cloth is punched with a metal hole cutter to provide a slightly tight fit with the grommet. Then the grommet, and its washer are assembled on the cloth; a grommet press is used to secure the assembly. The cloth can also be cut with an electrically heated knife which will actually melt the cut edges of the Dacron to prevent fraying.

Even the simplest workshop should have good measuring tools. A yardstick, a tape measure, a level, short rulers, and sharp pencils are musts if you plan to do your own construction. For more precise work, you should have a micrometer or, better yet, vernier calipers. Vernier calipers can be used to measure the outside and inside dimensions of parts, as well as hole depths up to 6 inches.

Tinsnips should be used to cut complicated shapes from sheet aluminum. There are special tinsnip shapes for specific jobs. For instance, long-handled, long-jawed tinsnips are used for straight cuts; shorter, curved-nose tinsnips, for curves. Left- and right-hand snips allow left or right access to curved lines.

If you wish to thread your own bolts, you have to use a thread-cutting *die*. If a nut or solid metal part needs a threaded hole, a *tap* has to be used. Use a tapered, starting tap at first, making sure it follows the centerline of the hole. Next use a less-tapered tap, and finish with a bottoming or *plug* tap. It is generally better to drill a hole and use a bolt instead of using the cumbersome method of tapping a hole for a screw; if a screw breaks, it has to be drilled out, and the hole retapped. If a bolt breaks and falls out, it can easily be replaced.

For cutting out complicated shapes, drilling cross holes, and accurate, irregular machining, a metal mill is required. A lathe is used for metal parts that are circular in cross section, such as end plugs, axles, etc.

Soldering and welding is difficult with aluminum because it oxidizes. These jobs are best left to experts who are used to aircraft work. A poorly made weld reduces the strength of the metal significantly. A blowtorch can be used, however, to heat the aluminum tube in order to harden it. Only certain types of aluminum can be heat-treated this way.

Riveting is another efficient method of fastening two pieces of metal together. Two basic riveting methods are employed by hang glider builders. The orthodox method is used when both sides of the structure to be riveted are accessible. If you wish to rivet two plates together, use a rivet that fits the holes snugly, and extends past both sides approximately ⅛ inch. Place the head of the rivet on a solid, large metal surface. Hit the center of the rivet's protruding shank with a ball-peen hammer, causing it to enlarge. Hammer the enlarged section until it forms a rounded bulb, locking the plates together.

The *blind rivet* method is fast, and makes a secure joint. The popular "*pop*" rivet, usually tubular, is placed over the stud of the riveting tool. The rivet is then hand-pressed into the hole when the handle is pumped up and down a few times. This pulls the far end of the rivet against the inside of the hole and locks the parts in place (Fig. 8-8).

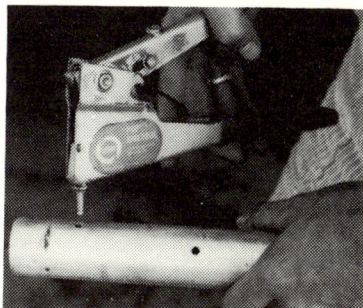

Fig. 8-8. The popular
Pop Riveting tool.

If you haven't had much experience with tools, ask a hardware salesman how to use the tools you are considering buying; or ask a tradesman to show you how even reading a book can be helpful. If you try your hand with scrap pieces, you will acquire the necessary skills rapidly. Always proceed slowly, and measure twice before you cut; it is much easier to change a measurement than repair an incorrectly cut or drilled part.

Having a well equipped workshop with a good light, sharp and well oiled tools, and an enthusiastic helper can add immeasurably to your enjoyment of the sport. Tune the radio to some nice background music, relax, and tinker your way from a collection of parts to a completed glider.

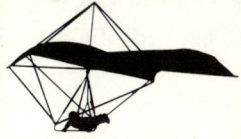

Chapter 9

Activities

In all sports there are doers and watchers, joiners and loners. During the preparation of this book, I met them all. Some pilots never had time to talk to me; they were always busy with something: flying, modifying, building, or organizing. Then there were watchers. Some were relatives, some were friends. Others, just passersby, stopped to watch, wishing they could fly, trying to work up the courage. I met members of several clubs, and subscribers to many magazines. I also met many who never belonged to any group and wanted no contact at all with others in the sport. Well, so be it; you can't force them. But it's hard not to tell them how they're missing out.

They are missing out on the excitement, the opportunities, and the fellowship awaiting the joiners and the doers—the devotees of hang gliding. For in this sport as in any other, the enjoyment is enhanced, the experience better savored, and the learning more fun, when you talk about it with others.

One of the pioneers of hang gliding, Dick Eipper, was farsighted enough in 1971 to call together the fellows who flew at Torrance beach. Twenty-five of them formed the Peninsula Hang Glider Club. The club grew rapidly and their correspondence with other people around the country indicated that hang gliding was growing around the world too. In 1972 the group expanded and called themselves the Southern California Hang Glider Association. They even published a monthly newsletter called the *Ground Skimmer*. (In those days they didn't soar so high.) The publication has been sent to thousands of interested people. By the end of 1973, interest in the sport had risen to the extent that the members voted to change the name of the organization to the United States Hang Gliding Association. Then, they had just over 5000 members. The year following, their numbers had risen to over 10,000. Today they're a nonprofit California corporation.

The USHGA is growing by 1000 members a month! Their purpose: to educate pilots and the public in the safety aspects of the sport; to study new equipment and techniques; and to make knowledge relating to these subjects publicly available. They also organize large-scale meets and publicize events in the *Ground Skimmer*.

The yearly membership fee is $12 (including a subscription to the newsletter).

Meetings are held every third Monday of the month at the Department of Water and Power auditorium, 111 North Hope Street, in downtown Los Angeles. You are welcome to join the more than 100 people there who conduct informal talks, have panel discussions, and show movies and slides.

Their large yearly meet used to be devoted to the memory of Otto Lilienthal. In 1973 the meet attracted nearly 300 pilots who brought 165 hang gliders. The first annual meet to honor Francis M. Rogallo was held in 1974, at which over 300 hang gliders were present. The USHGA nationals were held in the same year at Escape Country from October 1 to 6. Competition flights started at 1000 feet. The best two out of three flights were noted officially by five judges who also evaluated the pilot's overall style and his ability and judgment in achieving long duration, making maneuvers (a figure-8 and four 360-degree turns), and landing (safely). They were judging mainly the entire "flight system," rather than the pilot or the kite alone. The winner was awarded a $1000 first prize.

One of the important functions of the USHGA is the investigation of accidents which befall hang glider pilots. Their accident review board is paneled by several knowledgeable people, such as Mr. Wills (with 30 years experience in accident investigations), two doctors, several engineers, and manufacturers.

To encourage pilots to increase their experience and knowledge in the sport, the USHGA is setting up tests which will serve as an efficient indication of pilot skill. Tests have been given since 1973 in several distinct categories of difficulty. The HANG-1 test—named for the badge awarded—requires only one successful flight from no more than 35 feet, concluding in a perfect landing. The HANG-2 test requires three consecutive flights at not less than 50 feet. A HANG-3 badge is awarded for S-turns and other difficult maneuvers. The examination procedure is simple: a pilot with a HANG-5 rating or better has to verify the flights. HANG-6 is equivalent to a professional rating. Progressively higher levels are attainable by pilots who demonstrate excellence in judgment and skill in addition to flights of long duration, altitude achievement, and distance covered. The rating system is similar to that applied to glider pilots the world over. Hopefully, these badges will be recognized by the Federation Aeronautique Internationale, the body governing aviation, located in France. The HANG badges are actually decals which can be displayed on the helmet of the pilot.

The USHGA represents the hang gliding community at governmental proceedings and FAA investigations, and also helps newcomers to find others with similar interests the world over. Clubs are active in Hawaii, England, and New Zealand. The USHGA has a paid staff in its own office. Inquiries should be sent to: United States Hang Gliding Association, Box 66306, Los Angeles, CA 90066.

Hang gliding activity is picking up in Canada. Although Ontario leads the way in the number of pilots, Alberta has *two* magazines devoted to the sport. The *Updraft* is available from 35 Mill Dr., St. Albert, Alberta; the *The Flypaper* can be contacted at Box 4063, Postal Station C, Calgary, Alberta. Other nations have their own magazines and newsletters.

Most clubs and associations have their own official flying sites. The USHGA operates a site just north of Los Angeles near Sylmar. There is a full time flight director and hills suitable for beginning, intermediate, and advanced fliers. Launchings are made from 70 ft, 250 ft, 800 ft, 1400 ft, and 2500 ft.

Hang gliding contests may be quite informal, or formal, depending on the organizing club, the size of the area, and the

Fig. 9-1. Judges and announcer survey a recent hang glider meet at Escape Country.

number of contestants. I attended a contest recently at Escape Country, a park devoted to camping, motorcycling, and hang gliding, located near O'Neill Park, Mission Viejo, California. This site has complete facilities, including a hangar, flight school, several hills, and rest rooms. The event mentioned was fairly large; about 60 pilots competed. There were three classes: novice, imtermediate, and expert. All flew from the 500 ft hill. Each pilot was allowed three flights from which a total score was derived. The events were judged by four experts who watched the flights with binoculars and announced the results on the PA system (Fig. 9-1). The announcer decribed the pilot's background and kite while the contestant was in the air. Naturally, the spectators loved the colorful commentary. Four performance categories were judged: duration, bombing, safety, and style. For a flight lasting 45 seconds, 1 point was awarded; for 60 seconds, 4 points; for 75 seconds, 7 points; and for 90 seconds, 10 points.

During the bombing competition, each pilot carried a water-filled balloon, the "bomb," in his hand or between his teeth (Fig. 9-2). The target was a small, water-filled wading

A

B

Fig. 9-2. In "bombing" the competitor carries a water-filled balloon between his teeth.

pool which splashed when a bull's-eye was scored, surrounded by two concentric circles painted on the ground. A splash gave the pilot 20 points, while a hit in the first ring was good for 10 points, and a hit in the second ring earned 5 points. There *was*

Fig. 9-3. A spot-landing earns extra points for the competitor.

one hitch: a foul line painted as a circle 100 feet from the target. The pilot had to land within this circle (Fig. 9-3), or he did not receive any accuracy points at all. Five safety points were awarded to any pilot who landed on his feet, in the proper manner, with practically no forward velocity (Fig. 9-4). A crash landing *deducted* five points from the score.

The judges watched the style of the pilot during the entire flight. Turns, soaring ability, and judgment were evaluated; and up to 5 points which could be accumulated was 65 per flight. The entry fee was $3 on each day (Saturday and Sunday). A huge truck was provided to transport kites back to the starting point, making it easy to log three flights on each day.

Other clubs have organized contests with variations of these events, such as one for the greatest speed attained between two pylons 200 yards apart on a ridge, or the greatest number of 360-degree turns a pilot can complete in 2 minutes. The variations are almost endless.

I hope that the descriptions of these activities have made you eager to enjoy the obvious benefits of joining the club. But what if there is no club near your home? Start one! This may be easier than it sounds; once people hear of a new and inexpensive way to realize their dreams of flight, they come from near and far.

Suppose you have just returned from a California vacation and you were so excited about having seen the great, colorful kites, you bought one. Now you are back home, in an area completely untouched by hang gliding. You want to try the kite, but there is nobody else near you with similar interests. Well, that's okay; as soon as you take your kite out to the nearest hill, a large crowd will gather around you. They will have dozens of questions and, unless you are a complete loner, you had better be prepared to answer them. In fact, now would be a good time to take the names of interested people so that you can call them the next time you go out. Perhaps a newspaperman will show up; if you give him your name and address, he will no doubt publish the information in his newspaper. The day after the article appears, you can expect dozens of phone calls expressing interest in the sport. Most local newspapers will be glad to send a reporter to your flying site if you notify them a day or two in advance.

If you want additional publicity, make up some calling cards with a catchy phrase like "Want to fly like a bird? Call———." Put the cards on bulletin boards where you work, in Laundromats, in hobby stores, in sporting goods stores, and

Fig. 9-4. A standup landing adds extra safety points.

in supermarkets. In fact, if you attach a photograph to each notice (perhaps cut from a kite catalog) you should get good responses as long as the notices are up.

Soon you will have dozens of names on your list; then it will be time to call a meeting. Although the sport is basically outdoor oriented, it is best to have a place to meet indoors so the participants can be best heard. Try to find a hall with enough comfortable chairs to hold everybody. Some social clubs, banks, the American Legion, or similar organizations might be willing to rent you a room for a reasonable charge. Or they might just give it to you. You can collect donations at the door to help defray expenses. Set up your kite near the main table to focus the attention of the participants on hang gliding.

Start the meeting by introducing yourself and talking about how you became interested in the sport; your enthusiasm should be contagious. You need not be a public speaker to inspire people—just speak from your heart.

When the audience's interest is high, show movies or slides you have taken of hang gliding activities. When the lights come on, your audience should be ready to start flying. Now you have their attention—now is the time to start organizing. Pass out information. Most manufacturers will gladly send you stacks of information about their products, and it will cost you only a postcard. Some companies will even rent their publicity movies about hang gliding. Others, such as Chandelle, will send out an instructor-demonstrator, if you can guarantee a large turnout. Perhaps somebody also eager to found a club will propose a name for one. Decide on definite purposes for the club, and start drafting some rules. Nominate officers, and once the basic framework for an organization is achieved, sign up anyone who wants to become a member. Before the meeting adjourns, call the time and the place of the next meeting, perhaps outdoors.

At this point, the newly elected officers should sit down and discuss plans for the immediate future. It is best to appoint a chairman for the meeting and to follow Robert's Rules of Order (parliamentary rules) so ideas will be properly proposed and voted on. This saves time and tempers as well.

At this time you can also formalize the official positions in the club: president, vice president, secretary, treasurer, editor, and safety officer.

The president will represent the club in negotiations with agencies to obtain flight sites or to arrange contest dates with other clubs. During regular meetings, the president will present various items on the agenda and keep order in general. Since *you* called the meeting in the first place, don't be surprised if they nominate you for this position. The vice president should be prepared to substitute for the president whenever necessary. The vice president can also perform other tasks for the club.

The secretary will take accurate minutes of the meetings (what was said and what was decided). This person will also keep a roster of names and addresses of members. The secretary should be prepared to do a little typing and be present at the beginning of each meeting, promptly.

The treasurer is responsible for, and keeps records of, funds which come from membership fees, contest entry fees, and club sales. This person should open a club bank account nearby and have one of the other officers serve as cosigner. The treasurer is required to report on the financial affairs of the club at every meeting.

The safety officer will be entrusted to keep an eye out for safety hazards, unsafe equipment, unsafe flying conditions, and safe contest start intervals. His job will also include giving the flag signals and keeping in touch with those reporting weather conditions at faraway sites.

The editor's job is particularly important in keeping interest high. Even a one-page monthly newsletter does an excellent job of informing members about coming events, results of contests, goings-on in the sport, equipment for sale, and the activities of other members. No other single item can add to the life of the club more than a newsletter. The editor can solicit article ideas from members—descriptions of trips, pictures or sketches of equipment, new developments—or do most of the work himself.

It may be a good idea to consult a lawyer friend for advice on whether to incorporate. There is an element of danger to

Fig. 9-5. A trophy made by Dick Eipper to be awarded at yearly competitions for the most outstanding flight.

club members involved, and individual liability can be limited if the club is incorporated.

A club, with a treasury, can achieve many things that would be unattainable to separate individuals; for instance, a club can more successfully negotiate for a flying site. The club can have group liability insurance that will provide the site's owner with the peace of mind that comes with knowing that any damage to his property can be attended to by a reputable underwriter. For another thing, a club secretary, by using club stationery, can effectively negotiate for film rentals, help coordinate contests, and be heard by the United States Hang Gliding Association.

Club funds can be used to purchase PA equipment, a first-aid kit, film for motion picture studies, trophies (Fig. 9-5), even a hangar. The club may decide to purchase somebody's used but still good kite for instructional purposes or for rental.

Club life can be enhanced by organizing events not associated with actual flying. These events can be organized in the off-season, to keep the group together, or after flying sessions. Dances and socials can be held for fund-raising, and to provide an opportunity for fliers' friends to meet the other club members.

It may be a good idea to organize a swap meet once in awhile where members can exchange equipment or buy and sell hang gliders and accessories.

Fig. 9-6. The Harlan Derriere makes an excellent club project.

Fig. 9-7. Many flight schools in-
itiate the student with this "flying
seat."

With a large number of people around you interested in the
sport, you can overcome the inconvenience of being quite far
from hang glider factories by having someone in the club
become a dealer for a reputable manufacturer. (This might,
however, create a "one-design club" unless more than one
manufacturer is represented.) Having a dealer in your midst
is a sound idea because you can be sure of a good supply of
spare parts and new equipment. Most factories prefer to have
pilots as dealers instead of selling their wares in sporting
goods stores where no facilities exist for instruction or
personal followup. It is a good idea to write to all the
manufacturers to find out what programs they have to help
local clubs. Long winter evenings may be spent by club
members building a trainer plane or "club kite" (Fig. 9-6).
Club colors, T-shirts, etc. seem to foster team spirit. Make
sure, however, that you operate the club in a low-key,
informal-yet-safe manner to preserve hang gliding's personal
freedom.

As hang gliding grows by leaps and bounds, so does the
need for devotees and manufacturers to get together once in
awhile to discuss new products, equipment, and so on.

Fig. 9-8. Dealers and customers meet and discuss the finer points of flying and equipment at a hang glider show.

Recently I attended such a show held in Long Beach, California in the city auditorium. There were demonstrations of all kinds (Fig. 9-7) by flying schools and manufacturers. Each major manufacturer had displays where casual browsers were given brochures about hang gliding and products in general (Fig. 9-8). Clubs and associations

Fig. 9-9. Bill Bennett makes spectacular landing on parking lot at hang glider show held in Long Beach, Calif.

exhibited as well, their booths manned by the pioneers of the sport as well as the "big names" like Bennett, Valderrain, Brock, Miller, Eipper, and Colver. This was a golden opportunity for a novice to become really immersed in the excitement of this tremendous sport. In addition to the movies shown, live demonstrations were given. Bill Bennett's demonstration (Fig. 9-9) began with a car-towed launching; he flew between buildings and landed standing up, on a target laid out on the parking lot.

Shows of this type are being planned for various parts of the country and will soon be a yearly activity.

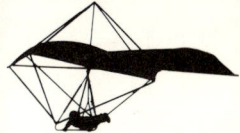

Chapter 10

Safety Aspects

No other single element affects the future of hang gliding and its public acceptance as much as safety. Technical advancements, new designs, and flying skill mean a lot to devotees of the sport; but these never make headlines in newspapers—accidents do.

Headlines which point out only the negative elements of the sport are sure to result in the revocation of permits for flying sites, public apathy and resistance, and federal regulations pertaining to licensing. It is of vital importance that hang gliding retains its image of a healthy, peaceful recreation rather than a daredevil, mankilling activity. From the first time you touch a hang glider, you should cultivate an attitude of safety.

Some safety techniques have been worked out by experts which should be considered by everyone concerned. While it is important that a pilot's weight be kept low, it is even more important that he wear some protective gear, especially during the learning period when landings may be not so smooth. Hang gliding, like any other kind of potentially dangerous activity, requires a protective helmet. The lightest helmet is the type worn by mountain climbers. It has a rim which reaches just below the ears. The conventional motorcycle helmet reaches too low, and is too heavy for hang gliding. Bell makes a very good helmet which is widely used by hang glider pilots (Fig. 10-1).

If a regular crash helmet is not available, you can use a football helmet. *In a pinch*, you can fashion a helmet from a

Fig. 10-1. All hang glider pilots should wear a safety helmet such as this short-neck model manufactured by Bell. (Drawing Courtesy Ultralight Flying Machines)

heavy plastic mixing bowl by lining it with foam rubber. Do not use a hardhat, it provides little protection in a crash because it has no chin strap, and it may be swept away during a flight. Your ears should be exposed to the outside (cut holes if necessary) because covered-up ears impair your sense of balance.

Surprising, very few pilots wear goggles. Wind velocities are seldom great enough to cause problems, although goggles would seem to have a beneficial effect when landng in heavy brush. The best type seems to be the all-transparent goggles used by sky divers.

Beginners should wear a light jacket, or at least a long-sleeve shirt; some landings may be on your stomach, and your arm can be scraped by bushes or rocks. If the weather is really cold, you may have to use a skin diver's wet suit. In any case, make sure that your garments fit tightly so that air drag will not impede your flight.

A good pair of boots is a necessity (Fig. 10-2). During climbing, when you carry the kite up the hill, you need the sure footing of a good sole. During landing, a pair of strong boots with high sides can be invaluable in preventing broken ankles. Even on the warmest day, I like to wear heavy socks to prevent sweaty feet, and to provide all-day walking comfort.

Fig. 10-2. High-ankle hiking boots are essential to prevent injuries.

A pair of gloves is very important during landings. If you are not skillful enough to execute a standup landing, your hands will touch the ground immediately after your feet. In fact, you may be scraping the ground for a considerable distance; need I point out further what the gloves are for?

Obviously, the kite you use should be safe. This means it should have been produced by a reputable outfit whose engineers designed the parts to withstand the stresses the kite will encounter. It should conform to the Category I specifications of the Hang Glider Manufacturers Association. Unless you are a flier with years of experience, you should not construct a kite. The most critical steps affecting safety are those taken immediately after assembling the kite at the site. Take a walk around the entire structure and inspect every joint (Fig. 10-3). Are the nuts on tight? Are pip pins all the way in? Are cables frayed? Are the aluminum parts bent or cracked? Is the cloth torn? Are the wires tight? Are the flying surfaces properly aligned? Is anything so worn or out of shape to be beyond use?

Now you are ready to buckle yourself into the harness or seat. Have a friend help because only he can see behind you. Make sure that all buckles, Velcro, and seams are in good

Fig. 10-3. A complete preflight inspection by two pilots is a must to prevent accidents.

shape. Fasten the harness to the kite securely; it's the only thing that holds you up during flight (Fig. 10-4). If anybody used the kite before you, make sure the balance is okay for *you*. I heard of a case where somebody fastened a movie camera to the keel behind the pilot and filmed his entire flight. Then, he took the camera off and handed the kite to the next

Fig. 10-4. What is wrong here? The pilot forgot to attach his harness to the kite! The result: the kite flew—the pilot didn't.

guy. Now minus the camera, the kite suddenly became extremely nose-heavy; it took the most vigorous and heroic maneuvers in the air to counteract the effect.

Fixed-wing gliders are especially tricky to rig because the proper alignment of all surfaces is essential to safety. After rigging, the pilot should sight along the centerline of the keel from the front of the plane to check for warped surfaces.

Always check the wind conditions at the site. If you are not familiar with the area, take a long walk along the hill, tie strips of canvas to trees, sticks, or bushes, and observe their position. It is quite possible that the wind direction on top of the hill will be different than that near the bottom. A smoke bomb, windsock, or a streamer can be used to ascertain wind direction (Fig. 10-5). Never fly when the wind is over 20 mph. It is best to fly when the wind is around 10 mph.

Check the landing site for hidden rocks, bushes, crevices, bulls, barbed-wire fences, etc. These cannot be seen from the starting point. Make sure there is a helper nearby to lend a hand in case of trouble, or at least to summon help should you need it. If you are under the influence of intoxicants or drugs that may impair your judgment to even the slightest degree, do not fly; your sense of balance and your strength will not be

Fig. 10-5. A simple streamer can be used to indicate wind speed and direction.

available when you need them. Remember your responsibility to those below you on the ground. Take off from only those spots whose height and terrain suit your capability, and which allow a good, safe run to gain speed. If you want to progress to a higher spot, check it out first with other fliers who can give advice based on experience.

All right—now you're in the air. Keep the nose of the kite level, or nearly so. Anything over or under 30 degrees from the normal flight attitude is considered dangerous. Always look ahead and keep a good grip on the trapeze bar. Never attempt to stand on the trapeze bar! One documented hang glider fatality was the result of a pilot who tried to show off by standing on the bar. A gust of wind caused him to fall through the triangle. He was unable to get back up—his weight put the kite in an extreme nose-down attitude which he was unable to correct. If you plan to do a complete 360-degree turn, make sure you have plenty of altitude—at least 500 ft. Turns towards hills are always potentially dangerous. With the relatively poor glide angle of kites, even a slight shift of wind or downdraft can play havoc with your flight path.

Good hills in hang gliding country are usually surrounded by several kites in the air, especially on weekends. What do you do when you meet other gliders in the air? Here are some rules that make as much good sense as those applicable to driving a car:

(1) The lower of two kites has the right of way. It is the responsibility of the higher pilot to avoid the other man.

(2) A pilot being overtaken has the right of way.

(3) When overtaking another kite below you, make sure your downwash does not affect his flight path.

(4) When approaching a kite coming from the opposite direction, keep to the right. If you are flying near a ridge, maintain your position relative to the ridge as soon as other kites enter the area; if you're right next to the ridge, stay there as long as it is safely possible to do so. Never do anything that will force another pilot closer to a ridge than the position he is maintaining there.

(5) The first man to enter a thermal determines the direction of rotation for other pilots who follow to avoid a head-on crash.

It has been proved, time and time again, that a hang glider being towed behind a land vehicle behaves very differently than it does in free flight. Several deaths have been attributed to towing hang gliders intended for foot-launching. Even being towed by a boat is difficult and dangerous; don't try it until you get some instruction from a flier who knows what he is talking about.

It should be pointed out here that flights over water are definitely unsafe. A landing in the water makes it difficult to get unhooked from the kite. You may be trapped under it and be unable to get out. Safety releases are available which will drop you from the kite should you decide you cannot possibly avoid a wet landing. If you're flying near water and haven't this sort of safety device, at least fasten floats to the trapeze bars and wingtips.

An extreme hazard is flying near high-tension wires or telephone lines. Also, avoid flying near buildings, water towers, or other manmade obstacles.

The Federal Aviation Agency has studied hang gliding with the view of possibly regulating it. Until this writing, no regulations have as yet been drawn; but the FAA has strongly recommended that the following safety suggestions be followed:

(1) Limit altitude to 500 ft above the general terrain. (Nevertheless, hang glider pilots should be aware that there are certain air operations conducted below 500 ft.)
(2) Do not fly within controlled airspace; specifically: airport traffic areas or within five miles of the boundary of an uncontrolled airport (unless authorized by airport authorities).
(3) Do not fly within the 100 ft radius of buildings, populated places, or assemblages of persons.
(4) Stay clear of clouds.
(5) Questions regarding operations in conflict with the above recommended safety parameters should be discussed with the nearest FAA office.

The FAA has also made recommendations to manufacturers, clubs, and persons using hang gliders regarding safety programs and protective clothing. The Hang Glider Manufacturer's Association (HMA) has given its assurance that their members will build kites to minimum performance and design criteria as a contribution to safety. To bring some order to advertising practices in the form of performance claims and specifications statements, the HMA has suggested the following requirements be met by its members before a kite is marketed:

(1) Demonstrate control at the extremes of the weight range for each kite size.
(2) Design kites with a glide ratio of at least 3:1 with the heaviest recommended pilot.
(3) Demonstrate recovery from a stall.
(4) Demonstrate a reasonably steep dive and recovery capability.
(5) Provide 360-degree turn capability.
(6) Demonstrate the kite's ability to make 90-degree turns.
(7) Demonstrate a landing accuracy of at least one success out of three tries at the center of a target.
(8) Demonstrate 8 seconds of hands-off flight without radical results.

Three HMA members must observe and certify the performance of member-produced gliders in accordance with the above criteria; an HMA member must fly the glider and pronounce it stable before it can be claimed to have met the Category 1 HMA standards. HMA has also worked out basic criteria for Rogallo-wing gliders. These appear in Appendix A.

To avoid any liability for accidents arising from hang gliding, most clubs, manufacturers, and park authorities require pilots to sign a disclaimer; copies of two popular forms are also reproduced in Appendix B.

I certainly hope that this chapter hasn't discouraged you from flying hang gliders. My purpose only has been to instill a sense of safety that will help everyone to see you as a sane, responsible pilot.

If the possibility ever materializes that large parks will be devoted to his sport, we may also have flying safety patrolmen who can get to an accident quickly and render help. Recreational parks today are helping the sport by providing safe launching and landing areas, a windsock, and a colored flag system to warn of adverse wind conditions. The system used by the Sylmar Flight Park near Los Angeles is a display of flags of four different colors, each with its own meaning. A green flag means the wind is steady at less than 15 mph; novice flying is permitted. Blue indicates 15 mph wind (plus or minus 5 mph); intermediate flying is permitted. A yellow flag warns that the windspeed is greater than 15 mph and gusts are present; no less than experts permitted to fly. Red, so widely recognized for danger, means: park closed; no flying permitted.

It is a good idea to appoint a knowledgeable person to act as a safety officer (Fig. 10-6). This person can also act as starter at the launch site to permit flying only when the wind conditions and landing area are safe. A bullhorn or PA system can be used to advantage. The safety officer should have the authority to stop anyone from launching who, in his opinion, is unqualified to do so. A classification system is now in use at Escape Country Flight Park. They classify as a *beginner*

Fig. 10-6. When many pilots use the same takeoff area, it is good practice to have a safety officer control traffic.

Fig. 10-7. A properly equipped hang-glider pilot: helmet, good harness, long pants, high boots.

anyone who has completed a recognized flight course. A *novice* is a person who has demonstrated safe flying from their 500 ft hill. *Intermediate* pilots are those who can show controlled flights from the 1500 ft level. An *expert* is any pilot who has demonstrated outstanding performance at flying contests.

In spite of safety precautions, there may be a time when you will be confronted with an emergency involving an injured person. I suggest you take an authoritative first-aid course to be prepared for such an emergency. There are a few simple yet very important points you must keep in mind to act as beneficially as possible when an injury occurs, if you haven't had such a course:

(1) Keep the injured person lying down. Loosen his clothing. Keep him cool or warm as appropriate; reassure him.

(2) Stop severe bleeding by applying pressure to the wound. A tourniquet should be applied only by an experienced person; by you, only as a last resort.

(3) If breathing has stopped, apply artificial respiration immediately. Do steps 2 or 3 as necessary to sustain life until the condition of the patient is stable.

(4) Do not move the patient unnecessarily, especially if a fracture is suspected. Immobilize the broken bone to prevent further damage, if necessary.

(5) Do not force liquids into an unconscious person.

(6) Keep onlookers away. Send someone for professional help.

(7) To prevent shock or minimize its effects, keep the injured person warm and as relaxed as possible.

Should an accident occur in your area, make sure that the person in charge is notified, and that all details of the accident are recorded and reported to the United States Hang Gliding Association. The USHGA gathers accident reports and analyzes each one to prevent similar accidents from occurring.

Chapter 11

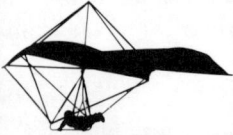

Model Hang Gliders

Most important airplane developments were first tried as models. Otto Lilienthal, the Wright brothers, Octave Chanute, and many other pioneers constructed small-scale replicas of their brainchildren to discover the basic rules which govern flight. Sometimes only the airfoil was tested; sometimes only the control system. Through the use of models the pioneers were able to arrive at simple rules of thumb before having to cut wood or canvas for the real thing.

Although an initial design may look good on paper, it's more economical to test it as an inexpensive model before a costly, full-size prototype is made. And even though stress calculations can be made beforehand, some structures may be so complex as to make it almost impossible to calculate forces with a great degree of confidence. Aerodynamicists today, working for manufacturers, have models constructed of new designs and test them in wind tunnels. Force gages are fastened to the various components of the model to ascertain aerodynamic pressures and stresses. Once the wind-tunnel model behaves in a predictable manner, a flying model may be constructed that is powered by a small gas engine and controlled by radio. Aircraft factories also make full-scale mockups to check the spatial relationship of the different parts. The National Aeronautics and Space Administration, and the National Advisory Council for Aeronautics before NASA, have conducted extensive tests with radio-controlled Rogallo wings, with and without engines. The idea was to develop a Rogallo wing which could be stored furled-up in a tube, dropped from an airplane, and erected in midair to land a payload safely and efficiently.

These techniques can be applied to hang gliders. New configurations can be easily duplicated in small scale and tested before a full-scale model is produced. Scientific reasons aside, constructing models of hang gliders is just plain fun. The younger members of the family can play with their models while dad and mom play with bigger versions.

Looking through modeling magazines, I found several articles describing the construction of hang glider models. There is an article on a *mini* hang glider by Bill Hannan in the March 1973 issue of *Junior American Modeler*. It is a small model; the keel is only 8½ in. long. The configuration is basically a Rogallo wing made from $1/16$ in. balsa strips covered with a thin plastic material such as that used for plastic-film dry-cleaning bags. A pilot, made from thin cardboard, hangs from old-fashioned parallel bars. There are no bracing wires or kingpost, making it simple to assemble in a couple of hours.

You have probably seen small rubberband-powered models in hobby shops and drugstores; Harold W. Warner, a Los Angeles teacher, has designed a Rogallo wing around one of these models. Instead of the conventional wing, Warner used a simple, plastic-covered triangular structure. The keel is 14 in. long, and construction is simple. Flights of several minutes are claimed; in fact one of the models flew out of sight. The designer was careful to point out two things: it is important to color the plastic sail with colored pens to make it visible at long distances; and the vertical center of gravity must be located precisely. The latter can be achieved by adding clay to the landing gears.

The April 1974 issue of *American Aircraft Modeler* contains an article about Dick Eipper's Flexi-Flier, a radio-controlled hang glider that is 3 ft long. A Mattel doll, with radio gear for internal organs, hangs from the control bar of the Rogallo-wing craft. The modeler guides the model by shifting the doll's weight fore and aft as well as sideways, with a radio transmitter. Plans for a radio controlled model of Vollmer Jensen's VJ-23 Swingwing appeared in the October 1974 issue of *Radio Control Modeler*. The model is an exact replica of the real thing; it has wing ribs, tail surfaces, and a

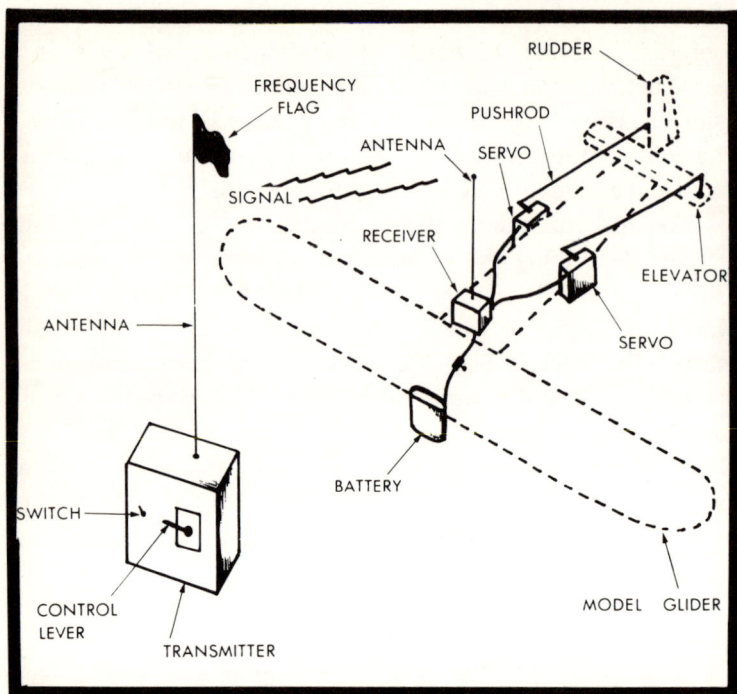

Fig. 11-1. A simple radio-control set consists of a transmitter, receiver, battery, and servos connected to the tail surfaces.

boom fuselage built from bits and pieces exactly like its larger counterpart. The pilot is a doll, weighted to provide the proper balance. The radio gear is inside the thick wing.

Radio control systems can be purchased from any well equipped hobby store. Each "set" is fully assembled, ready for installation in any model airplane, car, or boat. By radio "set," I mean a transmitter, receiver, servos, and battery. Let's discuss each component (Fig. 11-1) one by one.

The transmitter, about the size of a thick book, is held in the modeler's hand. There is a "whip" antenna protruding from the top, just like those atop walkie-talkies. A battery inside powers the electronic circuitry which generates a series of coded signals. There is a lever (or two) on top of the transmitter connected to a potentiometer (voltage-control device) inside. Moving the lever changes the outgoing signal slightly in frequency (spacing).

A radio receiver is located in the model. It also has a short antenna through which the transmitted signal is received. The signal is then amplified and directed to the various servos.

A servo is a small electromechanical device consisting of an electric motor with a small potentiometer mounted on its output shaft. The receiver on board the model feeds its own signal to the servo and is so designed that its signals and those of the transmitter must be matched at all times. When the transmitted signal is changed, the receiver causes the motor to turn, thus controlling the potentiometer also. The potentiometer causes the transmitter's signals to once again match the receiver's signals, and the motor stops. A small arm is attached to the motor that operates the doll in the model, causing it to behave like an actual pilot. When the modeler deflects the control lever on the transmitter ¼ inch, the servo output arm also moves ¼ inch.

Thus, the servo output arm serves as the muscle power of the pilot, he can be made to move the controls, shift his weight, lower the landing gear, or whatever. In most cases only two or three servos are needed, each with its own function and control lever on the transmitter. But as many as six servos can be operated by one transmitter.

The transmitter's frequency is controlled by a factory-installed *crystal* that resonates at its own fixed frequency. There are 20 frequencies which can be used. These allow up to 20 model airplanes to be operated simultaneously, each under its own control. However, if a modeler wants to launch his plane, he usually has to wait until others land to prevent radio interference from causing his model to crash. Each transmitting frequency has been assigned a combination of colors which appear on a flag to be flown from the transmitter antenna (Fig. 11-2).

Once you have seen a radio control set in operation, the entire system will appear quite simple to you. There is absolutely no electronic knowledge required and no examination has to be passed to be able to use the frequencies, although the FCC requires that you apply for license. The nearest address of the Federal Communications Commission office can be found under U.S. GOVERNMENT in your phone book.

FREQUENCY (IN MHZ)	COLOR CODE
26.995	BROWN
27.045	RED
27.095	ORANGE
27.145	YELLOW
27.195	GREEN
27.255	BLUE
72.08	WHITE AND BROWN
72.16	WHITE AND BLUE
72.24	WHITE AND RED
72.32	WHITE AND VIOLET
72.4	WHITE AND ORANGE
72.96	WHITE AND YELLOW
72.64	WHITE AND GREEN
53.1	BLACK AND BROWN
53.2	BLACK AND RED
53.3	BLACK AND ORANGE
53.4	BLACK AND YELLOW

Fig. 11-2. The frequency color code for radio-controlled models. Frequencies printed bold are to be used by amateur radio operators only.

In foreign countries it is usually the post office which exercises control over radio control operations.

If you want to learn about the basics of flight, amuse your friends, or simply keep your hands busy with things related to hang gliding, I recommend that you build a model or two. There is an excellent $1/6$-scale kit available of a Rogallo-wing hang glider complete with kingpost, control bar, and steel rigging wires. The model, called the Rogue (Fig. 11-3), has a span of over 3 ft. It can be assembled in 2 or 3 hours. The weight positioning can be adjusted as well as the curvature of the keel (called *reflex*) so that their effects can be studied by the analytical enthusiast. With a special bridle, one can even fly it as a kite on a string. The kit can be ordered from W. B. Products Co., 560 S. Helberta Ave., Redondo Beach, CA 90277. If you can find a few pieces of wood and some plastic around the house, you may want to design your own kite. I have

Fig. 11-3. The Rogue has a trapeze bar, kingpost, plastic sail, and full rigging. A doll can be attached for realism and proper weight distribution.

constructed several models using fiberglass arrow shafts for the basic frame, and plastic for covering. You can construct your own model quite easily with 4 standard 29½ in. shafts, some tape, and a dry-cleaning bag. The only tool necessary is a drill. To begin the project, drill a $1/16$ in. hole through one end of three of the shafts. These will be the keel and wing spars (A, B, and C in Fig. 11-4). Through two of the shafts already drilled, drill a $1/16$ in. hole precisely 19¼ in. from the first holes. The

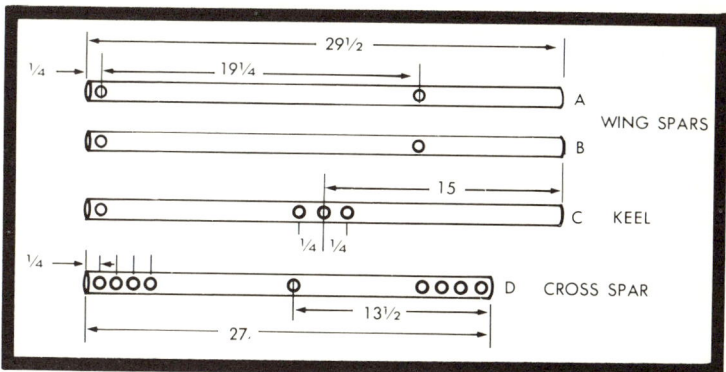

Fig. 11-4. Shaft dimensions.

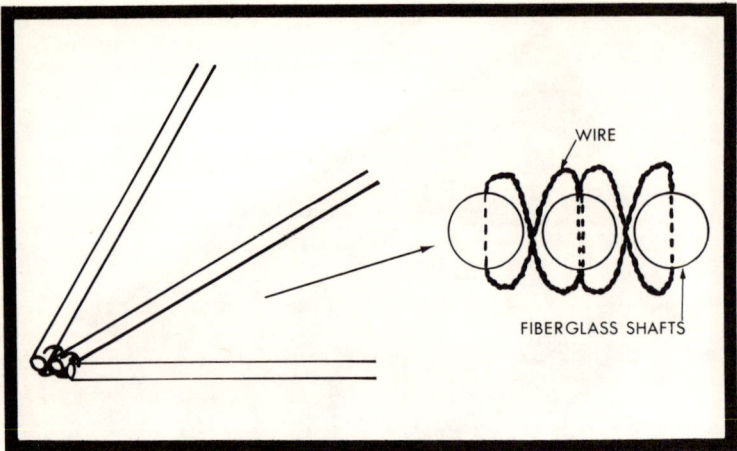

Fig. 11-5. Stringing the keel and wing spars together.

third shaft, with but one hole, will be the keel. The fourth shaft will have to be cut to 27 in. for the cross spar (D in Fig. 11-4). Eight holes are drilled in the cross spar (same drill bit), four at either end, each spaced ¼ in. apart beginning at each end.

Next, shafts A, B and C are tied together with strong string or thin wire that is threaded through the holes as depicted in Fig. 11-5. The three rods are then spread to an angle 45 degrees. A table corner can be used to verify the angle. Place the structure on top of a sheet of plastic (dry-cleaning bag), fold the edges over shafts A and B, and tack them down with cellophane tape (Fig. 11-6). But spare the tape for the time being to allow some room for adjustments. Fasten the cross spar (D) to shaft A and B in the manner used for the keel. Make sure that you use corresponding holes at either end of the cross spar for connects. More than one hole is used to allow adjustment of the wing-spar angle.

The sail will bulge when air fills the plastic. When you are sure that the bulge is even on both sides, add more tape to secure the plastic to the rods.

A piece of strong coathanger wire can be bent to form a control bar trapeze (Fig. 11-7). It should be attached to the keel and cross spar with string and tape as shown in Fig. 11-8. A ½ lb weight or "action doll" can be tied to the control bar to provide more realistic flights.

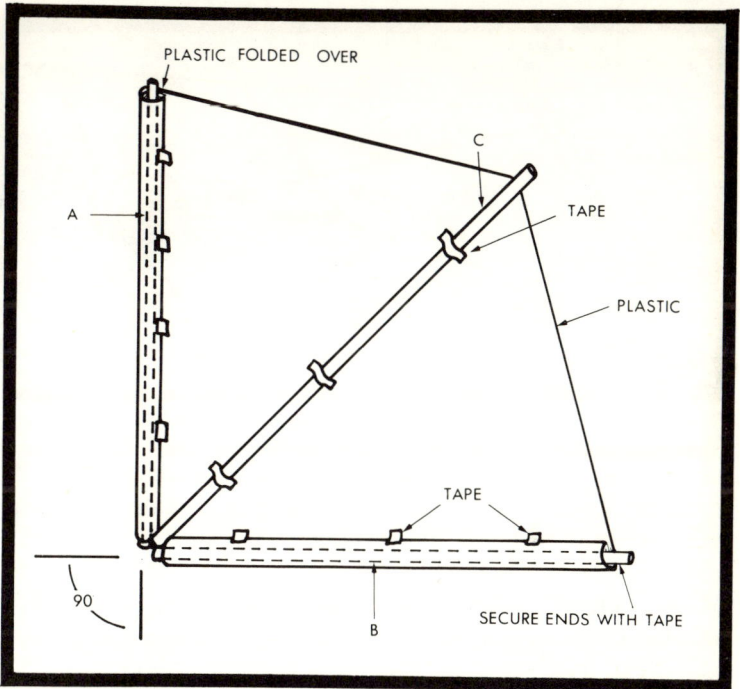

Fig. 11-6. After setting the wing spar angle, the sail is taped in place.

The glider is now complete and can be test-flown. Face the wind, let the sail bulge up and launch the model with a nice even, horizontal motion. If it dives into the ground, bend the control bar towards the rear of the keel or bend the legs of the doll so they point more backwards. This will place the center

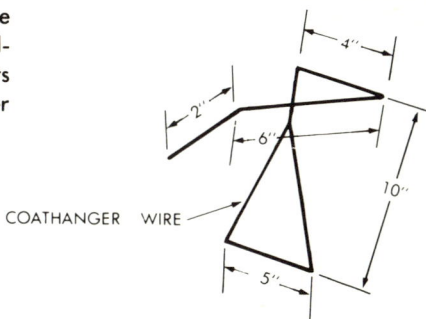

Fig. 11-7. The trapeze. It will be adjusted after flight tests for the correct center of gravity.

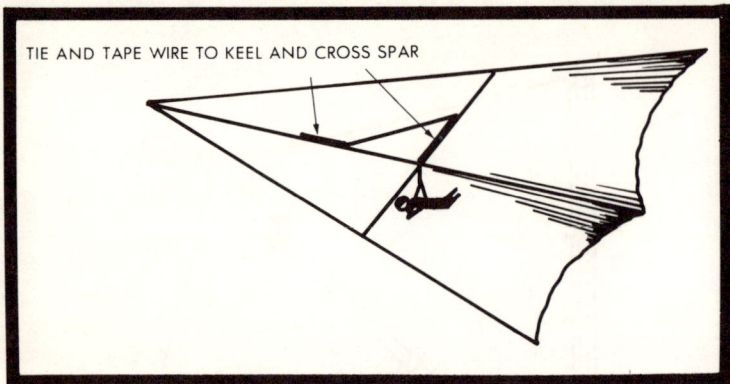

TIE AND TAPE WIRE TO KEEL AND CROSS SPAR

Fig. 11-8. Trapeze attachment.

of gravity to a more rearward position, correcting the tendency to dive. If the glider rears up and stalls, bend the wire towards the nose. If the glider tends to fly to one side, bend the wire towards the other side.

It is best to launch the model from a hill, facing the wind of course. After each flight, make sure the wire and the doll are put back into position. When the center of gravity is ascertained, threads can be added to the trapeze bar to lock it in place, much like the flying wires of a real hang glider. In fact, a kingpost can also be added, complete with ground wires. You will be surprised how much this model will teach you about the fundamentals of hang gliding. Proper launch speed and angle of attack can be demonstrated. The effect of weight-shifting will be dramatically evident. Unfortunately, points of high strain usually show up after you break the structure. The ability to achieve optimum sail shape without distorting the plastic will become second nature to you. After rough landings, points of high wear (such as where the plastic is joined to the wing spars) will show up—what you learn from such observations can be applied later on to the real thing.

Use holes at the ends of the cross spar for setting up various nose angles to control the bulge of the sail. You will learn about flight dynamics when you adjust the sail from a deep bulge to a shallow one. You can add more weight, change the shape of the control bar, install battens, and change the curvature of the keel; in general, you will have a lot of fun

Fig. 11-9. Simple models can teach you a lot. Clay can be used for nose weight. Experiment with sail curvature, nose angle, etc.

sailing the model. It will make long, straight flights when launched from a high hill into a gentle breeze.

Even if you only use cardboard to make a simple model Rogallo wing (Fig. 11-9) you will learn a lot. Use clay to weight the nose or shift the center of gravity. Adjust the wing curvature and nose angle. Model hang gliders are a ball.

Here are the addresses of modeling magazines from among which you can order back issues containing the articles mentioned:

American Aircraft Modeler—249 Freeport Blvd., Reno, NV 89510.

R/C Modeler—120 W. Sierra Madre Blvd., Sierra Madre, CA 91024.

Model Airplane News—No. 1 Broadway, White Plains, NY 10601.

Model Builder—1105 Spurgeon St., Santa Ana, CA 92701.

Sport Modeler—249 Freeport Blvd., Reno, NV 89510.

In England: *Radio Control Models and Electronics*—Box 35, Bridge Street, Hemel Hempstead, Herts, HP1 1EE.

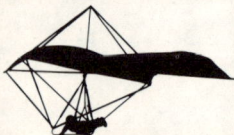

Chapter 12

Accessories

Any sport or hobby becomes more enjoyable with the acquisition of accessories for increased performance. In the beginning, hang gliding was a very simple activity. One only needed a hill and a kite, and the fun began. While the same is still true, today there are a number of accessories and devices which can add to your knowledge and enjoyment of the sport.

Glider seats have been long evolving from primitive beginnings. Hang gliders in the early 1970s used to have a simple parallel-bar arrangement. The pilot would stand between the bars (usually made of bamboo or aluminum), run into the wind, and when the kite rose in the air, lift himself up and place the bar below his armpits. This was true *hang* gliding. It was good enough for short hops lasting a few seconds. When the hops became flights of a minute or two, the parallel bars became very uncomfortable. Then some enterprising soul taped foam rubber to the bars.

When flights became long enough to be literally unbearable, some kind of seat had to be fabricated. Whatever the original prototype was, it did not take long before somebody remembered his childhood swing in the backyard. This early pilot simply took the seat off a swing and attached it to his kite. With the seat hanging from the frame by ropes, it was possible to run with the kite as well as sit in it. During flights, however, a seat of this sort threatened to slip from under the pilot. So the next logical development was a safety rope, attached to the seat to hold it in position right up to landing.

The simple and light *swing seat* is still very popuar among kite fliers. It is usually made from molded plastic and held to the kite by means of polyethylene ropes. It is important to remember that the seat must be properly suspended from the kite's center of pressure; the kite flier can then actually let go of the control, with the kite flying on undisturbed. Some kites have several suspension points placed about two inches apart on the keel. This allows one to find the best position for seat suspension before attempting hands-off flying. Sitting up and flying at a good speed, one feels a noticeable amount of air pressure—pressure that produces drag and reduces the glide angle; it was not too long before one of the early fliers suggested that a prone position might minimize the effect. Seats acquired a harness which allowed one to swing into a horizontal position immediately after becoming airborne.

The prone harness is quite similar to a parachute harness. While there are several variations, most of them employ wide webs (to reduce pressure on the body) around the waist, between the legs, and over the shoulders. The line which connects the harness to the kite is attached at the waist on either side. Because the waist corresponds roughly to the body's center of gravity; the body can be rotated around it. Some flyers use snaps or buckles to attach the lines to the harness; some pad the harness with foam rubber or thick fur to reduce the pressure on the body.

Some harnesses are really like vertical seat types in that they are attached with suspension lines to the shoulder and hold the flier much like a parachute harness. The conventional harness is usually attached permanently to the keel of the kite, but may employ a *carabiner* (a snap-hook used by mountain climbers) for attachment. While it takes but a few seconds to undo a carabiner after landing, this cannot be accomplished until the flyer's weight is taken off the lines. A safety buckle is available which can be undone in a fraction of a second by flipping a lever. This is a good feature to have should one want to abandon the kite in a hurry (e.g., to avoid a wet landing).

Flying in a prone position can be tiring because the flier has to support the weight of his legs. In the way of relief from this, there are harnesses which incorporate rubber straps

Fig. 12-1. Harness arrangement for prone flying.

attached to the legs and waist (Fig. 12-1). In flight, the straps supply the support, and their tension is adjustable to individual preferences. It is important to adjust all harnesses so that they do not encumber the movements of the pilot. If you are working in a harness of your own, suspend it from a hook in the ceiling for a test before you take it in the air.

Transporting kites is fairly easy with a carrying rack. The folded kite can be simply tied to a car-top rack. Most keels are so long that they will hang over the top of a car by a considerable amount (Fig. 12-2). During long drives, one runs

Fig. 12-2. Most pilots carry the folded hang glider on a simple car-top carrier with a stabilizing bar.

the risk of having the wind catch the sail cloth, causing it to stretch or tear. Unless a bag is used to store the kite in, such a disaster becomes a probability. Bags are available commercially, but they can be homemade from waterproof material; just make sure that the end facing the wind is made from extra sturdy material. A zipper, Velcro, or snaps may be used to hold the flaps of the bag down.

During long drives, especially on bumpy roads, the overhanging kite may bounce around so much that the aluminum tubes will bend. To prevent this, it is best to make a simple frame to support the extreme ends of the keel. I prefer an X-shaped frame, mounted on the bumpers (front and back), as a convenient cradle for the kite. The frame can be made from metal conduit or flat iron. It does not have to be very strong because it will be strengthened by the kite attached to it.

Walking with a kite on level ground is difficult if there is any wind; even without a wind, carrying 35 to 55 pounds is a chore. To make the task easier, some pilots attach a slender shaft to the control bar, the ends of which are equipped with wheels. The shaft runs parallel to the control bar and extends beyond the length of the bar by about 6 inches. With wheels in place (plastic or rubber) the kite can be left on the ground and pushed or pulled along. The plastic wheels are only adequate for short transport, while the rubber variety (Fig. 12-3) are

Fig. 12-3. Wheels mounted on the trapeze bar make carrying easier.

Fig. 12-4. A specially equipped truck can carry several kites.

beyond the length of the bar by about 6 inches. With wheels in place (plastic or rubber) the kite can be left on the ground and pushed or pulled along. The plastic wheels are only adequate for short transport, while the rubber variety (Fig. 12-3) are

Owners of flying sites, to help pilots using their hills, often convert large, flat-bed trucks for kite transport (Fig. 12-4). Folded kites are put on racks or bars on top of the truck. It is usually unnecessary to fasten the kites to the truck because trips are short and the pilots stand on the truck supporting their own kites.

The modern pilot can learn more about his sport and improve his skill faster with flight instruments. In the early days of flying, most pilots relied on their senses to tell them whether they were losing altitude or gaining it. They had to sense their speed by listening to the wind. The first primitive "instrument" for flight was a strip of cloth attached to one of the control bars. By watching the strip one could tell the direction of the wind before takeoff, and wind direction relative to the glider in the air. Even the airspeed could be judged to some extent with this simple indicator.

Today, speedometers and variometers are available to pilots. Mehil Enterprises makes an airspeed indicator (Fig. 12-5) that weighs just a few ounces and can be mounted in convenient view of the pilot. Housed in a black

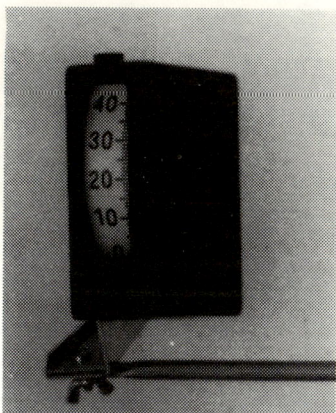

Fig. 12-5. The Mehil airspeed indicator.

anodized-aluminum case is a pivoted flat plate which deflects when onrushing air strikes it. The plate is connected to a meter marked with evenly spaced increments, allowing easily read indications. When the air is still, a weight on the plate returns the needle to zero automatically. A swing-down bracket is available for the unit so the pilot can move it out of viewing position when not in use (Fig. 12-6).

Frank Colver, a California inventor, manufactures a variometer for hang gliders. A variometer is a device which

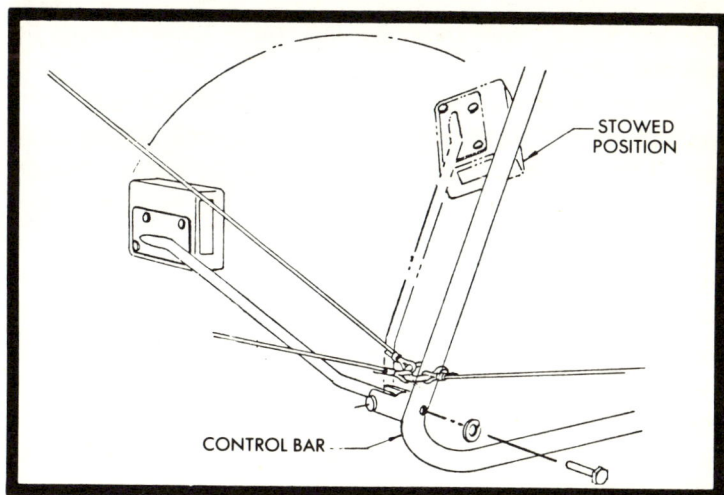

STOWED POSITION

CONTROL BAR

Fig. 12-6. The swing-down bracket gets the indicator out of the way quickly and easily.

Fig. 12-7. The Colver variometer.

indicates whether you are losing altitude or climbing. There is a small bottle in the device with its opening located just next to an electronic temperature-sensing device. When a glider climbs and the surrounding air pressure gradually diminishes the relatively higher pressure in the bottle causes air to slowly seep out of it. This is sensed by the temperature sensor which sends a signal to an amplifier and a speaker. The speaker emits a steady whistle in the absence of air leakage. The sound from the speaker rises in pitch when air leaks out of the bottle. When the glider sinks, air seeps into the bottle, and the sound from the speaker lowers in pitch. The device can be calibrated with a sensitivity adjustment.

The Dwyer gage is quite popular among hang glider pilots. It is a block of plastic with a tapered vertical bore containing a light plastic ball. Air enters the device at the bottom of the bore and escapes through the top. The ball rises in the bore in proportion to airspeed. It can also be used on the ground to sense the speed of the prevailing wind.

Altimeters intended for airplanes can be adapted to hang gliders. A surplus store would be a likely place to find one. Altimeters designed for cars, although not very accurate, can also be used. These gages usually incorporate a bellows to which the meter's needle is attached. As you go up and atmospheric pressure decreases, the sealed bellows expands and deflects the needle in the meter.

A slope gage can be made very easily that can tell you how the glide angle of your glider compares to the rise of a hill. Simply hang a weighted line from the center mark of the straight edge of a protractor. To use it, align the straight edge (curved side down) with the slope of the hill and note the smallest degree mark the line intersects. If the angular reading is greater than your glider's glide angle, a takeoff would be unsafe (Fig. 12-8).

No pilot should be without a log book. No matter how simple or elaborate you want it to be, it will be invaluable as a record of all the important factors pertaining to your flights. It can provide a record of your accomplishments, with signatures of witnesses, in case you are aspiring for a hang gliding emblem. Factors such as wind velocity and direction, altitude of takeoff point, flight duration, disability, etc. can be easily recalled for future reference. There might come a day when even hang glider pilots will have to "log" a certain number of hours to qualify for takeoff from certain high cliffs.

Some pilots even equip their kites with a squeeze-bulb horn. Horns are a lot of fun in the air when pilots honk at each other just for a laugh. But they have a more serious

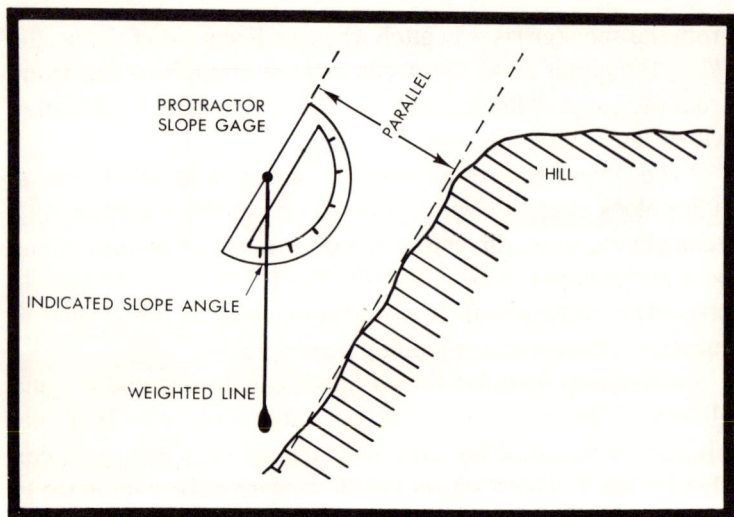

Fig. 12-8. A homemade slope gage. If the indicated slope angle is greater than your glider's glide angle, a takeoff would be dangerous.

application in warning unsuspecting bystanders of an impending touchdown (Note the horn in Fig. 12-3.)

A well run flying site is equipped to provide the utmost convenience for the fliers who use it. Some clubs have acquired an extensive array of equipment for their member's use. Some even have their own hangars, similar to that shown in Fig. 12-9. The hangar is used for storing gliders and equipment on days when the site can't be used. First-aid equipment, a snack bar, spare parts stores, an office and telephone, living quarters, and a repair shop might also be included. Even a simple shack could suffice if it were no less than 50 by 25 feet in size. The flat can be used for a judges' stand, or to accommodate spectators.

A hangar just isn't complete without a pole-mounted windsock or other wind direction indicator. In addition, a windspeed indicator may also be located there. Remote-reading indicators can be purchased for the site from electronics or department stores. Such indicators are electrically connected to a meter located in the hangar office. A full complement of instruments will also include a barometer (located in the office) and a thermometer. Such a

Fig. 12-9. Escape Country hangar offers full facilities.

facility gives the pilots as much information as possible about local atmospheric conditions.

While the essential hang glider relies on gravity and wind for motive power, attempts have been made to equip gliders with engine power. Rogallo wings have been made with tricycle landing gear, bucket seats, and engines. These

Fig. 12-10. Bill Bennett's one-cylinder engine with a three-bladed prop. The unit is carried on the pilot's back.

machines look much like home-built gyrocopters and do not really belong in the hang *glider* category.

Bill Bennett devised engine propulsion for a glider mounting a small one-cylinder engine on his own back. The engine had a conventional pull starter and a small gas tank. The throttle was connected to a lever on the control bar with a flexible bowden cable. A small three-bladed propeller was driven by the engine and housed in a wire cage for safety (Fig. 12-10). The whole contraption demonstrated some improvement in flight characteristics; but most of those who watched it had second thoughts. Yes, the idea was good; the execution, superb; and the feat, daring. But somehow the spirit of hang gliding, the silent floating through the air, the smell of clean air, seemed threatened as the spectators watched a trail of smoke following a noisy engine. I hope such contraptions remain engineering excersises only.

Appendix A
HMA Specifications for
Rogallo Hang Gliders *

SPECIFICATION 1—BOLTS

All Category 1 aircraft shall be equipped with aircraft type grade 5 or better bolts for all fastening applications. Grade 8 bolts are recommended. All bolts must be of proper length for the design application; i.e., the unthreaded portion of the shaft should take all loads. Threads should not extend below washer and nut. At least 1½ threads must show above the locknut when the fastener is in position and ready for flight. All bolts using wing nuts with secondary safety systems should have a hole in the bolt for a safety pin at least one thread above the fastener when in position ready for flight. Corrosion-resistant plating must be used on all bolts and fastening hardware. ¼ in. minimum bolt size is required for all main structural joints.

SPECIFICATION 2—NUTS

Locking fasteners are required on all critical—i.e., necessary for flight—joints. Nylon or plastic-filled locknuts are acceptable; however, metal locking types are recommended. Nylon nuts are to be used only on singular operations, i.e., where the fastener is used once. A secondary safety system, i.e., safety ring or safety pin, is required on all nonlocknut systems.

SPECIFICATION 3—CABLES

All flying wire cables must have a minimum pull-breaking strength of 920 pounds, i.e., equivalent to $^3/_{36}$, 7 × 7 stainless

---

*Approved by HMA membership at Grand Targhee. Wyoming. Thursday. 22 August 1974. (All specifications effective November 1. 1974.)

cable. Any cable other than stainless must be at least corrosion-resistant. Landing wires, i.e., cables connected to the kingpost, must be at least ⅔ as strong as those used for flying wires.

SPECIFICATION 4—CABLE ENDS

Both swaged and Nicopress fittings are HMA approved, provided they are installed in accordance with FAA manual AC 43.13-1A Chapter 4; e.g., single Nico sleeve application at the cable loop is approved; however, the cable must protrude through sleeve after swaging. In this event, some sort of covering similar to plastic heat-shrink tubing is recommended to prevent open cable ends from cutting or tearing the sail. Thimbles of corrosion-resistant material are required on all cable loops. NOTE: For home-built kits where proper Nicopress swaging tools are not available, it is recommended that two Nico sleeves be used on all cables rigged with hand operated swaging devices.

SPECIFICATIONS 5—SINGLE-LOOP CABLES

Single-loop flying wires of continuous strand are acceptable to both front and rear mounting points provided a properly swaged Nico sleeve is used to locate the flying wires at midpoint in the cable. A twist in the wires is recommended at the Nico sleeve mounting point to prevent undue load at the sleeve.

SPECIFICATION 6—TURNBUCKLES

No turnbuckle shall be installed on any flying wire without an approved secondary system being permanently attached. Such secondary systems must be as strong or stronger than the primary system. Approval for such designs must be secured in writing by the HMA technical committee. Standard hardware-quality turnbuckles are not permitted on any airframe. Only aircraft-quality or specially designed tensioning devices of corrosion-resistant material will be permitted. It is recommended that turnbuckles or tensioning devices be used only on the upper cables, i.e., landing wires.

SPECIFICATION 7—ATTACHMENT POINTS

Tangs or other such specially designed mounting hardware must sustain at least three times the pull strength of the attached cable or flying wire. It is recommended that all attached systems be made of corrosion-resistant materials.

SPECIFICATION 8—BALL LOCKPINS

All quick-release mechanisms are acceptable only when used in a shear load type application. Ball lockpins are not acceptable where the locking device must carry a load; i.e., the shaft must take the entire load. The recommended distance between the locking balls and the locking surface shall be $1/16$ in. minimum. Any hole next to the locking balls must be within the designed tolerance of the ball lockpin's manufacturer. All ball locks must lock against steel of a hardened-steel safety washer. Safety wires or lanyards are recommended to locate quick-pins near their appropriate mounting point.

SPECIFICATION 9—SAIL MATERIAL

Any wing or membrane material should be comparable in strength and wear characteristics to at least 3 oz "fleet boat" Dacron sail cloth; therefore, this eliminates monofilm polyethylene sails. Other comparable characteristics should include stretch and weathering resistance and long-term durability. Other materials may be submitted to the HMA technical committee for approval in writing before use in production. The best material for production use at the time these specifications were approved is 3.8 oz stabilized Dacron.

SPECIFICATION 10—STITCHING FOR SAIL MATERIALS

Thread and needle size must correspond to the sail-material manufacturer's recommendation. Either straight or zig-zag stitching is approved. Double stitching is recommended. Alternate methods of fastening sail materials are acceptable provided they meet the same standards for strength, wear, and durability as conventional methods and are approved in writing by the HMA technical committee.

SPECIFICATION 11—TUBING

The minimum size of 6061-T6 or 6063-T882 material for gliders over 14 ft shall be 1½ in. diameter with 0.049 in. wall thickness. Other sizes of similar or different material can be approved by the HMA technical committee upon submission of adequate test data for the use required. A minimum yield strength of 35,000 lb with characteristics comparable to or exceeding 6063-T882 or 6061-T6 aluminum is recommended.

SPECIFICATION 12

At any point where a connecting or fastening load is imparted to the airframe, e.g., wing spar to cross spar, an outer sleeve of similar material plus an internal crush-resistant material, such as a wooden dowel or bushing, is required. At any point on an airframe where a fastener is used for locating other structural hardware, e.g., nose plate, tangs, etc., an internl bushing is required and a dowel is recommended. Cross spar end holes must have crush-resistant bushings or dowels or their equivalent. Alternative systems can be submitted to the HMA technical committee for approval in writing.

SPECIFICATION 13

Some sort of vertical structure above, and connected to, the airframe is required to triangulate the airframe's main structure by use of "landing wires." Such structure or "kingpost" shall have triangulating wires going to the nose and tail longitudinally, and from wing-spar junction to wing-spar junction transversely. It is recommended that neither the kingpost nor "landing wires" interfere with the sail when the glider is in flight.

SPECIFICATION 14—CONTROL BARS

Because of size variations on different models, control bars do not have definite specifications other than the following: The minimum tubing size permitted in any control bar design shall be 1.0 × 0.065 in. 6061-T6 or the equivalent. Such tubing can be used only provided all flying wires are attached to specially designed fittings that can impart the flying wire loads equally into the tubing; e.g., no holes can be drilled for eyebolts or flying wire mounts in 1.0 × 0.065 in. 6061-T6 or its equivalent. In all cases, flying wires cannot attach to the control bar more than 6 in. from the base bar unless some additional structure is used to effectively double the wall thickness at that point. It is recommended that all bars be reinforced at the mounting points with additional internal or external sleeves of equal or greater wall thickness. On multisection control bars all connecting devices must be structurally stronger than the control bar material itself. The attachment systems on the base bar to the down tube structure must be such that a shear load of at least 750 lb can be applied to that junction without visual signs of stress. Furthermore, any control bar base tube must be capable of withstanding a 50 lb bending load. Bars are to be tested by mounting the bar at the point where the flying wires are attached and a 750 lb weight suspended in the center of the control bar. No visible deformation should be evident after the test weight is removed.

SPECIFICATION 15—PILOT SUPPORT SYSTEMS

All parts of pilot support systems used on Category I hang gliders must support at least four times the intended flier's weight.

Swing seats.—In the case of swing seat support systems, a continuous strand of the support systems material—webbing, nylon rope, etc.—must pass under the seat to insure the flier's safety in the event of seat breakage. All swing seats must have a quick-released lap belt with a buckle of the metal-to-metal type. Chest and back straps are recommended to prevent the flier from falling out of the seat. Should such a seat system possibly interfere with the wearing of a helmet, a "spreader bar" above the pilot's head is highly recommended.

Prone harness.—Variations in harness design preclude any definitive specifications; however, it is required that the vertical straps supporting the pilot from the mounting point on the glider be of a continuous-strand design around and under the flier to prevent the flier from being disconnected from the glider in the event of some harness failure. In general, it is recommended that any system used to support the flier have some sort of "easy release" system to enable the pilot to quickly detach himself from the airframe in an emergency. Furthermore, such a system should operate easily and in any attitude, whether a load is being placed on it or not. Should a "real" quick-release (i.e., instantaneous pull-release) system be used, it should have some sort of *positive* secondary safety system to prevent the flier from becoming totally detached inadvertently.

SPECIFICATION 16—SPECIFICATION PLATE

All gliders meeting HMA Category I specs must be equipped with a plate stating the fact. The HMA plate should be affixed to the glider's airframe where it can be easily seen by any flier, or meet inspector. It is further recommended that each glider have affixed to it a disclaimer warning clearly stating the potential hazards of flight in Rogallo-type aircraft.

Disclaimer wording as of August 22, 1974:

WARNING

Hangliding is a dangerous activity and can result in serious injury or death even when engaged in under ideal circumstances. This equipment is manufactured in accordance with the safety, material, construction and flight standards established by the Hang Glider Manufacturer's Association, Inc. This equipment should be used only under proper conditions after proper supervised instruction and practice from an experienced hang gliding instructor. The manufacturer has no control over the use and maintenance of this equipment and all persons using this equipment assumes all risks for damage or injury. The manufacturer and the HMA, Inc. disclaim any liability or responsibility for damages or injury resulting from the use of this equipment.

SPECIFICATION 17—INSTRUCTION BOOKLET

All gliders sold by HMA members must be delivered with an HMA approved instruction booklet covering the basics of Rogallo-wing flight. The list of such approved booklets is available from the HMA. Furthermore, it is recommended that each manufacturer supply a bibliography of readings with the booklet to further instruct the buyer in improving his flight techniques. The approved bibliography of readings is available from the HMA and shall be updated from time to time.

DEMONSTRATED FLIGHT CONTROL REQUIREMENTS FOR HMA CATEGORY I ROGALLO-TYPE HANG GLIDERS

The following maneuvers can be performed by either the factory fliers or by factory-assigned fliers. No glider shall receive HMA Category I approval without performing these maneuvers:

A. Demonstrated control by fliers both at the high and low end of manufacturer's recommended weight range for the glider.

B. Achieve a minimum glide ratio of 3:1 over a distance of 100 yards with the heaviest recommended pilot.

C. Demonstrate stall and recovery.

D. Demonstrate steep dive and recovery.

E. Perform two consecutive 90° turns in opposite directions.

F. Perform two 360° turns in opposite directions.

G. Demonstrate parachuting ability of the glider by landing on a 6 ft circle at least once out of three tries from an altitude of 300 ft.

H. Demonstrate 8 seconds of hands-off flight with no radical changes in attitude.

MAINTENANCE AND PREFLIGHT INSPECTION

It is suggested that all flying wires be replaced every 50 flying hours or after 6 months of flying and normal ground handling. Replace all worn components regularly; damaged parts, immediately. Flying wires should be replaced after any crash, as should any bent or damaged fasteners or hardware. Inspect entire airframe before every flight. Check all spars, sail, cables and their attachment points. Inspect all fasteners, hardware and secondary systems. Check control bar and pilot support systems for proper rigging relationship and wear. Be sure the glider is in correct trim per the manufacturer's specifications. Do not fly if the glider does not pass preflight inspection or if conditions are unsafe. Wear an HMA approved crash helmet.

Appendix B

Sample Liability Releases

I acknowledge that there are risks and dangers involved in using the facilities at the below mentioned location. I hereby release, acquit, and forever discharge their partners, owners, lessors, officers, agents, and all participants who might be using these facilities and location, from any liability, claims, demands, action, or right of action, whatever kind in nature or in law I may have or which may accrue in my favor or to my heirs, executors, or administrators, in any way growing out of, resulting from, or arising in connection wth my presence on, or in use of, this facility at this location, or on properties provided, should injury to my person, my death, or damage to my property occur within the confines of——however caused—whether by negligence or otherwise; and I hereby give consent to receive whatever medical care might be provided or be available on these premises. I also agree to conform to the rules and regulations of this facility. I, the undersigned, have read and understand the foregoing statements completely.

Signature _____

Date _____

Location_____

(This is a permanent liability release to be kept on file.)

SAMPLE RELEASE OF LIABILITY (FOR FLYING SCHOOL)

Whereas I am about to participate in the recreational sport of hang gliding and such participation is to include a course of instruction; and whereas I am doing so entirely upon my own initiative, risk, and responsibility; and whereas I recognize that hang gliding is an extremely hazardous and dangerous activity if engaged in improperly; I now, therefore, in consideration of the permission extended to me by the school, its officers and employees, do hereby for myself, my heirs, and executors, release and forever discharge the school from all claims, demands or actions on account of my death or injury which may occur from any cause during said activity as well as from all operations coincident thereto.

Signed _____

Date _____

Location _____ _____ _____

Appendix C

Directory of Organizations and Clubs

Boston Sky Club—Box 375, Marlboro, MA 01752.

Experimental Aircraft Association—Box 229, Hales Corners, WI 53130.

Michigan Association of Ultralight Flight—,c/o Grant Smith, 2597 Kingstone Dr., Walled Lake, MI 48088.

Midwest Hang Glider Association—c/o Al Signorino, 11959 Glenvalley Dr., Maryland Heights, MO 63043.

Northern New Mexico Free Air Force—Box 81665, San Diego, CA 92138.

Oregon Hang Glider Association—1729 Labona Dr., Eugene, OR 97401.

Self-Soar Association—Box 1860, Santa Monica, CA 90406.

Soaring Society of America—Box 66071, Los Angeles, CA 90066.

Southern California Hang Glider Association—Box 66306, Los Angeles, CA 90066.

Ultralight Flier's Organization—Box 81665, San Diego, CA 92138.

United States Hang Glider Association—12536 Woodbine St., Los Angeles, CA 90066.

USHGA Hang Badge Program—,c/o Jana Buehner, 340 Idaho St., La Habra, CA 90631.

Wings of Rogallo—c/o Gary Warren, 502 Barkentine Lane, Redwood City, CA 94065.

NOTE: Most of the organizations and manufacturers have local representatives. Please write to the address given for the name of the representative in your area.

Appendix D
Aeronautical Publications of Interest

Skysurfer Magazine—Box 375, Marlboro, MA 01752.

Hang Gliding—48 Walker St., N. Quincy, MA 02171.

Man-Flight Magazine—Box 90762, Los Angeles, CA 90009.

Ground Skimmer—11312 Venice Blvd., Los Angeles, CA 90066.

Hang Glider—3333 Pacific Ave., San Pedro, CA 90731.

Hang Glider Business Weekly—Box 1860, Santa Monica, CA 90406.

Delta Kite Flyer News—Box 483, Van Nuys, CA 91408.

Low and Slow—Box 1860, Santa Monica, CA 90406.

True Flight (book)—1719 Hillsdale Ave., San Jose, CA 95124.

Hang Flight (book)—Eco-Nautics, Box 1154, Redlands, CA 92372.

Simplified Performance Testing for Hang Gliders (book)—c/o Jack Park, 15237 Lakeside, Sylmar, CA 91342.

Guide to Basic Rogallo Flight (book)—Flight Realities, 1945 Adams, San Diego, CA 92116.

Updraft—35 Mill Dr., St. Albert, Alberta, Canada T8N 1J5.

The Flypaper—Box 4063, Postal Station C, Calgary, Alberta, Canada.

Helios—34795 Camino Capistrano, Capistrano Beach, CA 92624.

Motorgliding—Soaring Society of America, Box 66071, Los Angeles, CA 90066.

Model Aeronautics Made Painless (book)—c/o Frank Zaic, Box 135, Northridge, CA 19324.

Hang gliding movies are available from Delta Wing Kites, Box 483, Van Nuys, CA 91408.

Useful information on hang gliders and related subjects can be obtained from the following sources:

U.S. Government Printing Office, Washington, D.C. 20402

MIL SPECS—Commanding Officer, Naval Publications Center, 5801 Tabor Ave., Philadelphia, PA 19120

Locknuts—ESNA Corp., 2330 Vauxhall Rd., Union, NJ 07083

Sailmakers supplier—Howe and Bainbridge, 816 Production Pl., Newport Beach, CA 92660

Appendix E
Magazine Articles for Reference

Bill Cox, "Icarus 11—How to Beat the High Cost of Aviating," *Private Pilot*, April 1972, pp 22—26.

Don Dwiggins, "Do It Yourself Aircraft," *Popular Planes, 1972*, pp 63—65, (Published by *Plane & Pilot*).

Don Dwiggins, "Hang Ten with the Sky Surface," *Plane and Pilot*, March 1972, pp 38—41, 57.

Dave Esler, "Move Over Birds, The Hang Gliders are Here," *Air Progress*, (Part 1), December 1972, pp 40—47, 76—79; (Part 2), January 1973, pp 52—59.

Russell Hawks, "Happy Birthday, Otto Lilienthal," *National Geographic*, February 1972, pp 286—292.

Bruce Glassner, "If Birds Can Fly, So Can I," *Gallery*, December 1972.

Taras Kiceniuk, "Icarus, A Modern Hang Glider," *Sport Aviation*, August 1972, pp 24—26.

John McMasters, "Eco-Flight is Here," *Lifestyle*, February 1973.

Richard N. Miller, "What About the Hang Gliders?" *National Aeronautics*, Spring 1973, pp 64—67.

Jim Spurgeon, "You Can Soar Like a Bird," *Argosy*, June 1973.

Wayne Thomas, "How To Build a Hang Glider," *Mechanix Illustrated*, April 1973.

John Underwood, "A New Look At An Old Sport," *Sport Aviation*, April 1973.

Paul Wahl, "Hang Gliders," *Popular Science*, June 1972, pp 92—94, 130.

"The Flyingest Flying There Is," *Reader's Digest*, February 1974.

"Fly like the Wright Brothers for $50," *Science and Mechanics*, June—July 1974.

"Icarus 11," *Sport Aviation*, August 1972.

Appendix F
HMA Members

CALIFORNIA

Sunbird Ultralight Gliders
1411 Chase St., No. 7
Canoga Park, CA 91303

UP, Incorporated
137 Oregon St.
El Segundo, CA 90245
(213) 322 7171
Pete Brock, Pete Leger

Dyna-Soar, Inc.
3518 West Cahuenga
Hollywood, CA 90068
(213) 876 6615
James F. Sommers

Manta Products
4465 Lincoln Ave.
Oakland, CA 94602
(415) 536 1500
Kent Trimble

Solo Flite, Inc.
930 West Hoover
Orange, CA 92667
(714) 538 9768
Robert Follman, Mike Miller

Hawk Industries
5111 Santa Fe, Suite 1-A
San Diego, CA 92109
(714) 272 7449
Burke Ewing III

True Flight
1719 Hillsdale Ave.
San Jose, CA 95124
(408) 267 0692
Herman Rice

J. L. Enterprises
1531 Lago
San Mateo, CA 94403
(415) 592 3613
Jim Lynn

Sports Kites, Inc.
1202 C E. Walnut
Santa Ana, CA 92701
(714) 547 1344
Bob & Chris Wills

Omega Aircraft & Kite Systems
Box 1671
Santa Monica, CA 90406
(213) 395 4991
Joe Faust

Seagull Aircraft
1554 Fifth St.
Santa Monica, CA 90406
(213) 394 1151
Mike Riggs, Bob Keeler

Free Flight Systems, Inc.
12317 Gladstone Ave.
Sylmar, CA 91342
(213) 365 5607
Gerald M. Albiston

Eipper-Formance, Inc.
1840 Oak St.
Torrance, CA 90501
(213) 328 9100
Steve Wilson

Delta Wing Kites & Gliders, Inc.
Box 483
Van Nuys, CA 91408
(213) 785 2474
Bill Bennett

COLORADO

Sailbird Flying Machines
3123-A N. El Paso
Colorado Springs, CO 80907
(303) 475 8639
Joe Sullivan

Sun Sail, Ltd.
Airport Business Center
6753 E. 47th Ave.
Denver, CO 80216
(303) 321 8482
Ted Schmiedeke, Brian Jensen

Chandelle Sky Sails
511 Orchard St.
Golden, CO 80401
(303) 278 9566
Don Stern

CONNECTICUT

Zephyr Aircraft, Inc.
911 New London Turnpike
Glastonbury, CT 06033
(203) 633 9074
Alfred Mulazzi, Richard Gilmartin

ILLINOIS

Apollo Sky Sailing Centers, Inc.
722 Barrington Rd.
Streamwood, IL 60103
(312) 885 0958
David G. Koch

KANSAS

Pliable Moose Delta Wings, Inc.
1382 Caddy Lane
Wichita, KS 67212
(316) 722 0981
Gary Osoba

MASSACHUSETTS

Man Flight Systems, Inc.
Box 375
Marlboro, MA 01752
(617) 485 5740
Mike Markowski

Sky Sports, Inc.
Box 441
Whitman, MA 02382
(617) 447 3773
Ed Vickery

MICHIGAN

Foot Launched Flyers
1411 Hyne
Brighton, MI 48116
(313) 229 8328
Dale T. Frey

OHIO

Chuck's Glider Supplies
27000 Royalton Rd.
Columbia Station, OH 44028
(216) 236 8440
Chuck Slusarczyk

OREGON

The Nest Airplane Works
1445½ W. 11th Ave.
Eugene, OR 97402
(503) 342 2276
Bernard Nolfard

TEXAS

Kondor Kite Company
Box 603
Lewisville, TX
(214) 434 1646
Spence Nelson

WASHINGTON

Sun Valley Kites, Inc.
17360 Beach Dr. NE
Seattle, WA 98155
(208) 622 3511
Bruce Barr, Jerry Miller

CANADA

Muller Kites, Ltd.
Box 4063, Postal Station C
Calgary, Alberta
T-2-T 5M9
Canada
266 1446
Willi Muller

Index

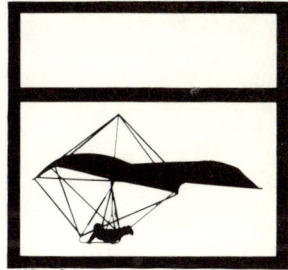